INTEGRATED ONLINE LIBRARY SYSTEMS:
PRINCIPLES, PLANNING AND IMPLEMENTATION

by David C. Genaway

Knowledge Industry Publications, Inc.
White Plains, NY and London.

Professional Librarian Series

Integrated Online Library Systems: Principles,
Planning and Implementation

Library of Congress Cataloging in Publication Data

Genaway, David C., 1937-

    Integrated online library systems.

    Bibliography: p.
    Includes index.
    1. Libraries--Automation. 2. Information storage and
retrieval systems. I. Title.
Z678.9.G45   1984   025'.04   84-15406
ISBN 0-87629-092-7
ISBN 0-86729-091-9 (pbk.)

Printed in the United States of America

Coypright © 1984 by Knowledge Industry Publications, Inc. 701 Westchester Avenue, White Plains, NY 10604. Not to be reproduced in any form whatever without written permission from the publisher.

10   9   8   7   6   5   4   3   2   1

Table of Contents

List of Tables and Figures iv
Preface v

1. Overview of Integrated Online Library Systems 1
2. Planning for an IOLS 15
3. System Evaluation and Selection 31
4. System Implementation and Acceptance 51
5. The IOLS Vendor Survey 65
6. Profiles of Integrated Online Library Systems 81
7. Microcomputers and Integrated Online Library Systems 111

Afterword: Trends in Integrated Online Library Systems 119
Appendix A: Survey of Selected Integrated Online Library Systems .. 123
Appendix B: Directory of Suppliers 135
Selected Bibliography 143
Index 147
About the Author 151

List of Tables and Figures

Figure 1.1: Non-redundant Single File Configuration 8
Figure 1.2: Redundant Multiple File Configuration 9
Figure 1.3: Non-redundant Multiple File Configuration 11
Figure 1.4: Non-recurring System Set-up Adlib Schematic 12

Table 2.1: Comparison of In-house Development vs. Purchase 20
Table 2.2: Comparison of Purchase Options 22
Figure 2.1: Youngstown State University Library Survey of
Attitudes Toward IOLS 25

Figure 3.1: IOLS User Survey 49

Figure 4.1: Vendor-Client Responsibilities 53
Figure 4.2: Sample Implementation Schedule 62

Figure 5.1: Survey of Integrated Online Library Systems 71

Figure 6.1: BASIS Integrated Institution System 85
Figure 6.2: LIAS System Diagram 103

Figure 7.1: Relationships between Computers and Storage Devices 112
Figure 7.2: Card Datalog Acquisitions Module 116

Preface

The purpose of this work is to provide an overview of integrated online library systems and to outline some of the planning procedures, evaluation and selection criteria useful in acquiring and implementing these systems. It is intended for all those involved in the selection and acquisition of such a system as well as all others interested in integrated online library systems.

The working definition of an integrated online library system is a system that accesses a common machine-readable database and has two or more subsystems operational and online or, more succinctly, a multifunction integrated system sharing a common database. For purposes of definition, circulation, acquisitions, online public access catalog, reference, documents, serials, cataloging, etc., are considered subsystems of a total library system.

Most integrated systems today are minicomputer based. However, this book will also briefly discuss microcomputer-based library systems, micros as interfaces and backups to larger systems, and potential future integrated systems.

SURVEYS CONDUCTED FOR THIS BOOK

Several surveys were used to obtain information for this work: an administrative survey of staff attitudes, an operational status survey of vendors' systems and a survey of system users.

Administrative Survey

In the early stages of planning for a system at Youngstown State University (the author's home institution), a broad spectrum of system options available emerged. The choices did not fit into precise little boxes, but sometimes overlapped, reflecting several administrative issues. An internal survey of librarians was devised to determine staff attitudes toward administrative issues involved in the selection of an integrated system. Once the philosophical orientation of the staff was determined, the types of systems that would receive the most serious consideration were then selected. This administrative survey of staff attitudes and its results are presented in Chapter 2 as a guide for other librarians.

Vendor Survey

In examining the various library systems it also became apparent that reality needed to be divorced from prophecy. When a system is installed, all subsystems and functions deemed essential should, at the very least, be operational. Delayed development can be tolerated in nonessential subsystems or functions.

It was discovered that making assumptions about any of the offerings of a vendor can set the library up for a very disappointing surprise once the system is installed. It cannot be assumed, for example, that because a system has a circulation subsystem it has an online public access catalog or vice versa. Further, the existence of a circulation system does not mean that it can do all the functions or operations presently performed in your library.

These experiences led to the development of an operational status survey to separate what is available now from what is in development or is planned. One of the most significant components of this book is the results of this comprehensive survey of more than 30 vendors of integrated online library systems. These findings are presented in tabular form in Appendix A. The vendors were queried by mail, telephone and in person. Information was also obtained from corporate literature.

There are a number of newsletters that report on new developments in integrated online library systems. These include *Library Systems Newsletter, Library Hotline, Advanced/Technology Libraries, Library Hi-Tech* and *Library Hi-Tech News.* Early issues of *Library Currents* contain concise paragraphs on integrated library systems. *Library Technology Reports* has devoted entire issues to various subsystems. James E. Rush and Associates recently issued a new series called *Library Systems Evaluation Guides,* which provides basic descriptions, addresses and contacts for each system as well as a method of evaluating the various systems. A looseleaf update service entitled *Microcomputers for Libraries* is also available on a subscription basis. (See the Bibliography at the end of this book for full citations.)

Because of the fast changing nature of library systems, the reader should *always* contact the vendor for the latest information on any system that he or she is interesteed in. If a circulation subsystem or acquisitions subsystem is attractive, but other subsystems are not yet operational or do not contain features being sought, check with the vendor before making a decision. These features or subsystems may either have been recently developed or may be under development. Although the system should be considered as a whole, the subsystem that is prime for your institution should also be prime in your consideration and evaluation.

User Survey

A survey of 70 users of major integrated online library systems was conducted to determine the degree of user satisfaction with integrated systems in general. The survey does not attempt to evaluate specific systems, but rather, provides some indication of the areas that users are most and least satisfied with. The survey and its results are discussed in Chapter 3.

SOURCES OF FURTHER INFORMATION

This book is a logical outgrowth of several previous works dealing with library subsystems alone. There have been several excellent works dealing with the component subsystems of a library, but few have addressed the total concept of a multifunction integrated system sharing a common database, or the broader aspect of treating the library as a total system encompassing and interrelating each subsystem.

Some other works should also be consulted by the serious researcher for more specific information on each subsystem. *Automating Library Acquisitions: Issues and Outlook*, by Richard Boss, and *Automated Circulation Systems*, by Alice H. Bahr, are two good examples of works dealing with specific subsystems. Others are *Public Access to Online Catalogs*, by Joseph R. Matthews; *Online Public Access Catalogs*, by Charles R. Hildreth; *The Online Catalog: Improving Public Access to Library Materials*, by Emily Gallup Fayen and; *Online Catalog: the Inside Story*, edited by William E. Post and Peter C. Watson. (Full citations for these and other works appear in the Bibliography at the end of this book.)

This book is the outgrowth of the author's experience as a library administrator with the responsibility of selecting an integrated online library system for Youngstown State University. Additional information and perspective came from the Conference on Integrated Online Library Systems conducted by the author at Columbus, OH, in September, 1983. This was the first national conference dealing with the integrated online library concept. Participating consultants, practitioners and system developers presented papers ranging in subject from an overview of systems to the evaluation, selection and implementation of specific systems.

Caveat: The ultimate selection for the Youngstown State University library should neither be considered an endorsement of one system over another nor a reflection on vendors not chosen. Any system chosen by a library will simply be the most appropriate and most expedient system for that institution at that time within the given constraints. Each organization will have local needs and priorities on which it must base its decision. Even within the same organization, the decision of which system to choose may differ at various times or stages of institutional development.

ACKNOWLEDGMENTS

Several persons and organizations deserve acknowledgment: Laura Cavanaugh, who assisted in data gathering, and Jim Rush, who served as a reader; the various vendors for their time and patience in responding to the survey and for use of their material for illustrative purposes; the users who responded to the survey; authors who laid the foundation with subsystem "building blocks"; my wife Inez (also a professional librarian) who, in addition to preparation assistance and proofreading, provided the moral encouragement and pleasant, stable environment conducive to the production of this work; and finally, my daughter Sharon, who has been suspiciously cheerful in tolerating her father's retreat to the lower office.

I would be remiss if gratitude were not also expressed to Adrienne Hickey, Senior Editor of Knowledge Industry Publications, and Karen Sirabian, Managing Editor, for their excellent suggestions and editorial assistance.

1

Overview of Integrated Online Library Systems

A new era in library automation has begun. It is marked by rapidly increasing computer power, mass storage capability and instant global communications. These events are causing an evolution in the concept of library automation. It began with the mere automation of manual processes, but is now beginning to go beyond this "manual mentality" to conceptually new applications and directions that will have a significant effect on the perception of a "library" and library work. The integrated online library system, which has eluded library automators for two decades, is becoming a reality in the 1980s.

EVOLUTION OF LIBRARY AUTOMATION

The concept of integrated library systems has its grey beginnings in the unit card with overtyped entries, one of the earliest attempts to use a common database for multiple access points. With the advent of the computer, the card file began to give way to the machine-readable database, ushering in the era of library automation.

Pioneers in Library Automation

In general, library automation has been evolving in a sporadic, unsystematic way over the past two decades, accelerated by developments in communications and computer capabilities. In the 1960s some libraries began to develop in-house automated subsystems, usually in circulation. Punched cards with unique, fixed field record formats were used to input and store data. The absence of a standardized format for bibliographic data both limited the exchange of software and caused it to become hardware specific.

Integration of library systems was a goal of early in-house automation efforts. In the late 1960s and early 1970s, Paul St. Pierre and Edward Chapman promoted the idea of looking at the library as a total system with various subsystems such as acquisitions, cataloging, circulation, etc.[1] However, such efforts were stymied by the limitations and expense of existing technology. As Richard De Gennaro stated in 1976, ". . . It can be said with considerable justification that the ultimate goal of library automation in the 1960s, the development of a total integrated system for a single library, appears to have been abandoned or at least set aside in the 1970s. . . . However, there are indications that the advent of powerful and inexpensive minicomputers and storage capabilities will lead to the revival of this concept in the next few years."[2]

Six major institutions pioneered in-house library automation efforts in the 1960s: Harvard University, New York Public Library, University of Toronto, Northwestern University, University of Chicago and Stanford University.[3] Two survivors of the early stage of library automation are the University of Chicago and Northwestern University (whose system has been in existence since the late 1960s).

At the beginning of the 1970s, the libraries that pioneered in the construction of in-house automation with unique formats found themselves with systems that were out-of-sync with the national, and increasingly universally accepted, MARC communications format. In addition, both software and hardware were quickly becoming obsolete as the result of developments in the computer and library world.

Introduction of MARC

The introduction of the MARC communications format, developed by the Library of Congress (LC) in the late 1960s, standardized formats and allowed a combination of fixed and variable length records, not readily handled by key punched cards. The development of MARC was as significant as the unit catalog card once was, since machine-readable records could now be reproduced, transported as tapes or transmitted as records and used by all libraries once local data were added. Originally limited to monographs, this format has evolved into MARC II for audiovisual materials, maps, manuscripts, scores, serials and sound recordings.

Rise of Networks

This single, standardized format for the transmission of bibliographic library data fostered the development of regional networks with databases of generic records.

These networks provided the large database of library cataloging information, much like the National Union Catalog, that had a standard format (MARC) and was accessible online. Some of the regional networks, such as OCLC, evolved into national utilities that served several regional networks. Libraries could now share the cost of cataloging their materials by accessing a common source for bibliographic data. As a result, more and more libraries converted their card catalogs into machine-readable form. Once machine-readable, the data could then be used as the basic data file for a large number of library operations.[4]

Though the initial application of network services was in cataloging and reference subsystems, promises of future subsystems and modules began to emerge. However, most libraries did not have access to sufficiently sophisticated hardware or software to provide for the complexities of the MARC format.* Thus, manipulation of the machine-readable data was limited.

Database Services

The emergence and rapid growth of the number of vendors of online database services, such as BRS, Dialog and SDC, fostered interest in interactive online searching. The online database vendors began to demonstrate the potential value of a machine-readable file beyond that of merely a mechanized shelflist or card catalog by using the full capabilities of automation to provide Boolean search strategies, full-text searching, etc.

The database services provided online access to hundreds of databases and thousands of records in a fraction of the time that it would take to search a library's holdings manually. Further, increasingly sophisticated software and search techniques were developed to improve access to machine-readable files. However, major computer manufacturers did not discover libraries as a market until fairly recently, concentrating instead on the more profitable business and commercial sector. Therefore, libraries are just now beginning to apply these techniques to their own machine-readable files.

Concept of Integrated Online Library Systems

Historically, each automated library has built its own local data record at its own location. As interfaces and linkages between different library systems become more available, access to an individual library's holdings will become easier for other libraries.

In the past, too, libraries have been nicely compartmentalized with separate sections for acquiring, processing and retrieving items. When automation has occurred, with few exceptions it has been limited to a given department or section, such as acquisitions or circulation. Earlier computer capabilities just did not seem to allow for it to happen any other way.

Presently, there is a clear trend away from automating bits and pieces or single subsystems toward integrated systems in which all subsystems (acquisitions, cataloging, circulation, etc.) are interrelated and share a common database. This interrelationship may not

---

*It is significant to note that a little-known software package developed by the Information Systems Office of the Library of Congress provided for in-house manipulation of a MARC format database in the early 1970s. BIBSYS, as it was called, was one of the best kept secrets of the library world, even though the software existed. A magnetic tape version was available from NASA via the Computer Software Management and Information Center (COSMIC) at the University of Georgia in Athens for a modest price (documentation was $26 and the tape was available for $1300).[5] A software package linking LC's in-house version with the communications MARC was still required, but could have been readily developed locally. Though quite dated by now, earlier application of this package could have fostered the development of integrated systems by providing access to the MARC database. This package included Boolean subject searches of MARC library tapes.

always be a physical one, but at least it seems so to the user. Although there are few systems available today that include *all* library subsystems (one or two components, most frequently serials control, are lacking), this situation will soon change.

WHAT IS AN IOLS?

While the concept of an integrated online library system has been evolving in the library world for some time, the term itself has not come into widespread use until recently.

Origin of the Term

The term "integrated online library system" has not appeared as a subject heading in *Library Literature* indexes as of this writing. "Integrated shelving, integrated collections" and "ISIS (Integrated Scientific Information System)" appeared as early as 1970. The specific term "integrated library system" appears to have had its origins in the National Library of Medicine (NLM) where it was used as the name of its library system in the late 1970s. NLM used the term in 1980 to describe a "minicomputer system in which all automated library functions are processed against a singlemaster bibliographic file."[6] (The term is currently a registered trademark of NLM, as is the abbreviation "ILS.")

In October 1982 the Association of Research Libraries (ARL) defined the term "integrated library information system" as "a single function database . . . composed of bibliographic data as well as other data necessary to carry out library related functions (e.g., vendor files for acquisition purposes, or borrower files for circulation)" and with all functions "fully interactive with each other."[7] Pat Barkalow, a coordinator of a panel on integrated systems at the 1983 Library and Information Technology Association (LITA) conference, felt that the definition of "integrated . . . as any automated system that combined more than one library function or more than one physical library" was too broad.[8]

The term "integrated online library system" was first used in 1983 by the present author in connection with the first national conference of the same name to more adequately describe the total concept of an online interactive library system.

Definition of an IOLS

The working definition of an "integrated online library system" as used in this book is *a library system that uses a common machine-readable database and has two or more subsystems operational and accessible online*. It is a multifunction system sharing a common database. Acquisitions, cataloging, circulation, public access catalog and serials are considered to be subsystems of the total library system.

Although this appears to be a relatively clear definition, there were some difficulties in applying it precisely when selecting the systems to be included in this book. For example, some systems have several machine-readable index files instead of one. These systems generate a separate subject file, author file and title file, and then pull these fields together to make a bibliographic record. Other systems adhere more to the classic definition. These systems have only one bibliographic file containing full bibliographic records that is searched each time a query is entered and from which partial or complete records are displayed.

Thus, the definition includes all systems that access and build upon a common database that is either a single physical file of bibliographic records or a simulated (virtual) record file constructed from separate index files.

Yet another problem with applying the definition is the rapidly changing nature of system development. A single subsystem, such as a circulation system, may be developed into an online public access catalog subsystem and acquisitions subsystem within a few short months. Hence, the working definition has been stretched somewhat to include systems that are likely to have two or more subsystems operational shortly, even though they may only have one available at the time of this writing.

This book attempts to be inclusive and to deal not only with existing integrated online library systems, but also emerging integrated online library systems. The emphasis is on systems that are or have been available for purchase from either the vendor or the developing institution. Proposed systems or in-house systems not currently available have been omitted.

The Ideal System

The following is a brief, oversimplified example of how an ideal integrated system would function:

• When bibliographic information is needed for acquisitions, all available data are entered into a terminal, a bibliographic utility is searched and copy for that title or a nearest match is displayed;

• If the title is not in the network database, a workform is displayed with all entered information on it;

• The information is automatically checked online against standard publishers' files (*Books In Print,* etc.) for verification;

• The exact or closest match is again displayed and more complete data are added to the record;

• All available information is recorded on the workform from either the network file or the book vendor and is dumped into the library's own database;

• If the searcher is an acquisitions librarian, and the item sought is not in the library's holdings, purchase orders are generated;

• When the book arrives additional information is added to the record;

• Cataloging personnel then call up the same record and add local data information such as call number, copy, branch, item code identification, etc., and indicate that the copy is ready for circulation;

• Patrons from on-site or remote locations search the public access catalog via author, subject, title or virtually any term or field in the record and discover whether the work is on order, in process, on a reshelve cart or in the stacks ready for circulation;

• Circulation calls up the same record when the item is checked out;

• The same file is used to record serial holdings and generate claims for items not received within a stated time period;

• When items are withdrawn the same record is called up and deleted or made to indicate that it has been withdrawn;

• The patron is able to know the status of a title at any time in the process.

Unfortunately, this simple, seemingly uncomplicated, ideal system has generally eluded the library world with few exceptions until the past two years, although interface devices and linkages with utilities and book dealers are fast making it a reality.

DEVELOPMENT OF INTEGRATED LIBRARY SYSTEMS

Early Systems

"The Integrated Library System (ILS): Systems Overview," a report published in 1981 by the Lister Hill National Center for Biomedical Communications, notes that in the mid-1970s the Washington Library Network (WLN) had developed a statewide integrated library system as part of its network.[9] Other large-scale integrated systems efforts during this period were Northwestern University's NOTIS III and IBM's Dobis/Leuven. Stanford University and the University of Chicago were also early pioneers; however, their systems were too costly to operate in a single library environment.[10]

It is interesting to note that several of the groundbreakers in integrated library systems and some of the current innovators (Georgetown University School of Medicine and Washington University Medical School) are medical libraries. The University of Minnesota Biomedical Library's IOLS was operating on a minicomputer system as early as 1972. Since it was implemented in machine language, before higher level languages became popular, it was very equipment specific and data processing personnel were needed to conduct any maintenance or make changes.

The advent of minicomputers greatly fostered the development of integrated online library systems. These lower cost systems brought powerful computing capability to libraries, many for the first time. Microcomputers could further revolutionize integrated online library systems and make them available to smaller libraries at a more local level (see Chapter 7).

IOLS in the 1980s

With few exceptions, there has been a lacuna of total integrated approaches to library systems in the past two decades. Few libraries have performed the classic systems analysis, evaluation and design or redesign advocated by Chapman and St. Pierre in 1970.[11] Many advances have come about through networks, commercial developers of turnkey systems or database vendors. Only very recently have commercial integrated library systems been developed. Claremont College was one of the first libraries to market an integrated library system to a bibliographic utility, OCLC. OCLC introduced this system with its local data system in 1982; however, it was marketed as a local library system, primarily limited to special libraries.

The first real cluster of integrated library systems began to emerge in the early 1980s, with the notable exception of the Dobis/Leuven system which was available in the late 1970s. It is worth noting that, until recently, these systems have generally emerged from the corporate sector, although some have been an outgrowth of federal funding, such as NLM's ILS and Data Research Associate's (DRA's) Library for the Blind. CL Systems, Inc. (CLSI), a commercial firm founded in the early 1970s, was one of the early developers of a turnkey circulation system. Quite logically, CLSI became one of the first commercial vendors to offer other subsystem modules that relate to a single database.

IOLS Clusters

Today, available systems seem to group themselves in clusters, with common sets of characteristics chiefly associated with their origins and primary applications. There is the academic cluster relying heavily on exhaustive records in MARC format, large storage capacities and inter- and intra-institutional resource indentification and sharing of holdings. The public library cluster needs to accommodate multiple copies and locations and is somewhat reliant on MARC format. The medical library cluster (MARC-based) is derived from the NLM system and is usually split into two main subsystems: one accessing its national serials database network (PHILSOM) and the other the local monographic database.

The special library cluster is not as concerned with MARC format and offers a wide degree of variation on the theme of integrated library systems. Where the academic and public clusters are more likely to have an integrated database, the special library sector is more likely to have an integrated system, even though there may be multiple databases.

All of these generalizations are somewhat risky and subject to variations within each cluster. However, they should provide useful background, particularly when a library is examining the origins of the system it is considering, as discussed in Chapter 3. Similarly, it is helpful to review the basic principles of operation of the integrated online library systems available today.

IOLS PRINCIPLES OF OPERATION

Although the basic principle of operation for an IOLS is simple—many different functions in each subsystem working off of a single machine-readable file of bibliographic

8   INTEGRATED ONLINE LIBRARY SYSTEMS

records—there are several variations on this theme. Central to all functions of an IOLS is file organization. Essentially, there are three basic principles of file organization for all integrated online library systems available today. The plans for these systems are illustrated in Figures 1.1, 1.2 and 1.3. (Keep in mind that these are greatly simplified diagrams and many combinations and variations exist.)

Non-redundant Single File Configuration

The Non-redundant Single File Configuration (see Figure 1.1) is an example of the classic perception of an integrated library system—a single file system. There is one central file containing all full bibliographic records. All searches (author, title, subject, etc.) pass through each record in the file to find the required items. Acquisitions retrieves the basic record from the database and creates the record in the format of this master file. Cataloging adds information to the record and corrects it if necessary. Circulation uses the same file for inquiry and possible tagging to indicate circulation status. The online public access catalog queries this same file to find the bibliographic records that match the search parameters entered.

Although there are many other factors governing the speed of processing—such as the total disk capacity of a system, the speed with which the computer can execute commands, the language level the program is written in—this arrangement could result in longer, less efficient searching. If all the records in the database must be searched each time any part or field of a record is sought, it could take more search time. On the other hand, when a

Figure 1.1: Non-redundant Single File Configuration

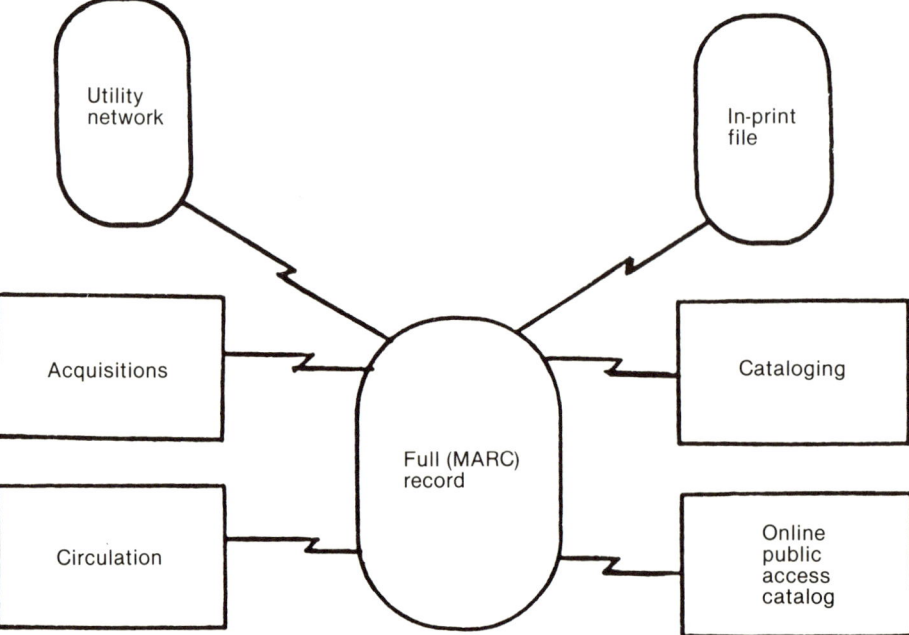

subject heading for a given record is found, the full record could be displayed much more quickly.

Redundant Multiple File Configuration

Redundant Multiple File Configuration (see Figure 1.2) illustrates a dual file system. In this system, the master bibliographic record file is still maintained. In addition, several files are created from it to facilitate some of the functions. A circulation file is spun off that contains only the fields essential to circulation, such as call number, author, title, etc. A separate subject headings file is generated with either minimal bibliographic information under each subject heading or with a record identification code that will allow the computer to find the full record if necessary. Obviously, subject searches can be conducted much faster with this type of file organization as opposed to searching an entire full-record file. Retrieving the full record may take a little longer than with the single-record file.

Figure 1.2: Redundant Multiple File Configuration

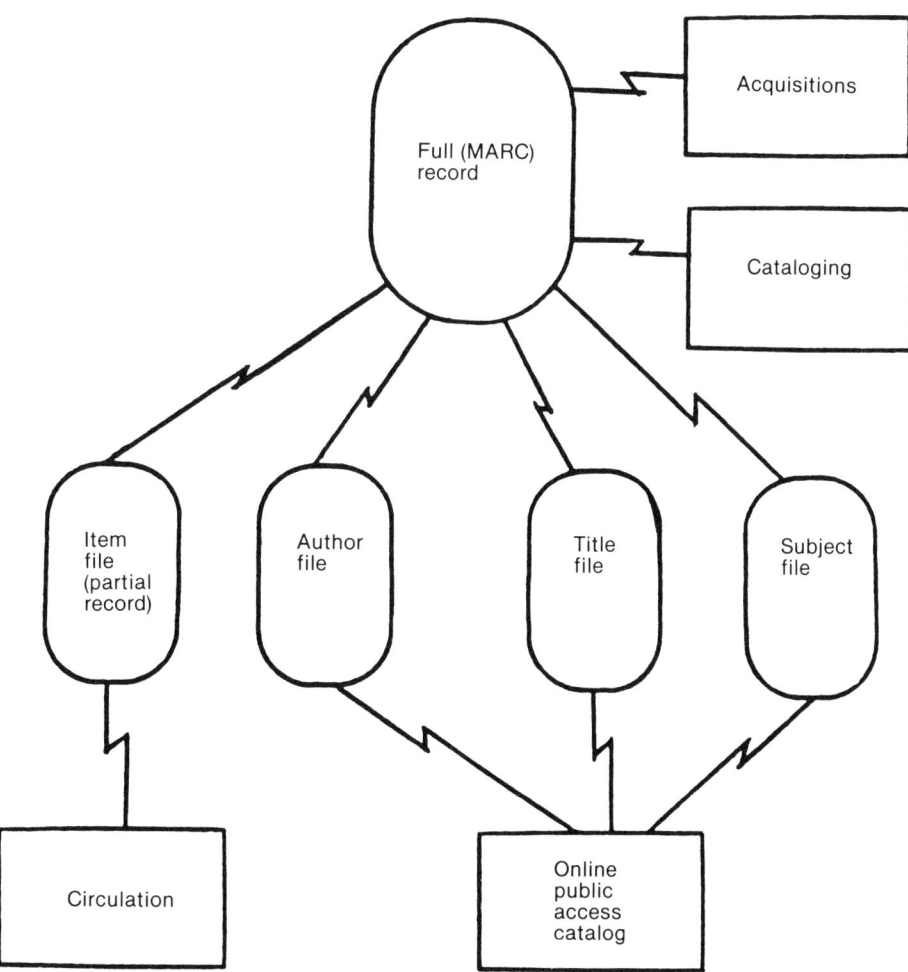

Keep in mind that "longer" or "shorter" retrieval time may not be really significant. The difference may be in milliseconds. Further, the speed with which items are retrieved, or at which the system operates, is also a function of the memory word size, computer architecture, computer language, etc. Usually, the larger the word size (32-bit versus 8-bit, for example), the lower level the language (i.e., the closer it is to machine language), the faster the computer will execute programs. The higher the language level, i.e., the closer it is to English, the slower the computer will execute programs. Thus, there are several variables other than file structure, although it is important, that can affect the rate of speed with which the system will operate.

Non-redundant Multiple File Configuration

The Non-redundant Multiple File Configuration creates a virtual or simulated master record file (see Figure 1.3). Here, the original or MARC record is split up into its main component parts or fields. Each separate file (author, title, subject, etc.) contains only that portion of the record and possibly an abbreviated record. Linkage is provided through control numbers. When the full record is called for, the computer quickly obtains all other fields from the various files through the linking code or number and constructs a virtual, or apparent, full record. The whole process is completely transparent to the user. Access time to any record in any of the separate files is considerably reduced. Viewing the entire record may take longer, since it must be reconstructed.

Example of a Specific System

Figure 1.4, LMR Information Systems' Adlib Schematic, provides an illustration of how the schematic presentation of one total integrated online library system, incorporating authority files and other files, looks. Note that although this set-up most closely resembles the Redundant Multiple File Configuration, there are some variations. Acquisitions is provided for through the "system administrator" terminal. One need not understand all the specific function acronyms, although most are fairly clear, to grasp the concept of the organizational structure.

Librarians should use these principles as a guide when examining different systems (see Chapter 3).

SUMMARY

Various developments in the evolution of library automation have contributed to the realization of the goal of integrated online library systems. Just as the unit card, with its transportable and standardized format, facilitated the growth of the shelflist and card catalog, so the MARC format, with these same characteristics, facilitated the machine-readable catalog and shelflist.

Networks, with their mass storage of MARC records, became the new "LC card division" where bibliographic records could be ordered via dedicated telephone lines. This allowed the development of tapes, and eventually disks, of local data records. Database

Figure 1.3: Non-redundant Multiple File Configuration

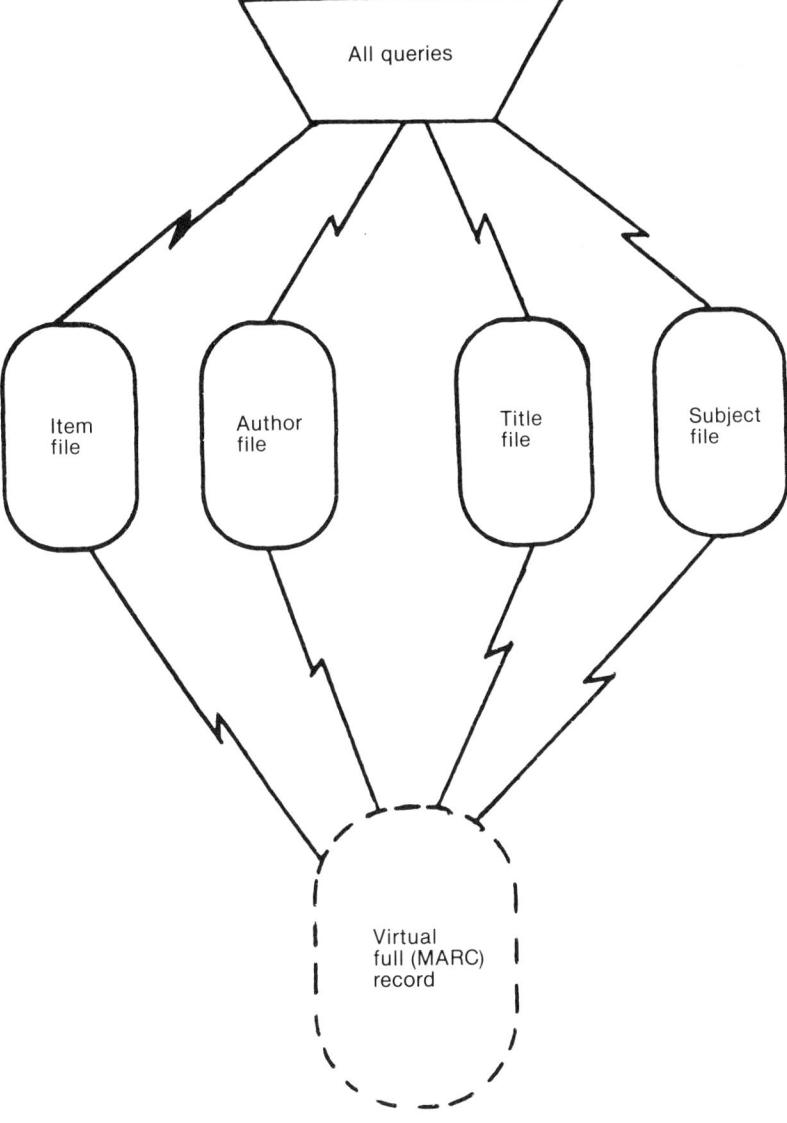

vendors gave librarians a glimpse of the potential of searching a machine-readable interactive shelflist vis-a-vis the catalog and stretched librarians' vision beyond mere mechanization of manual operations.

Few of the pre-MARC pioneers survived, with the exception of Northwestern and the University of Chicago. NLM was one of the first to operate an integrated library system. During the past two decades, only a few other libraries approached the library as a total system, with integrated subsystems and modules using a combination of online shelflist and public catalog.

12 INTEGRATED ONLINE LIBRARY SYSTEMS

Figure 1.4: Non-recurring System Set-up Adlib Schematic

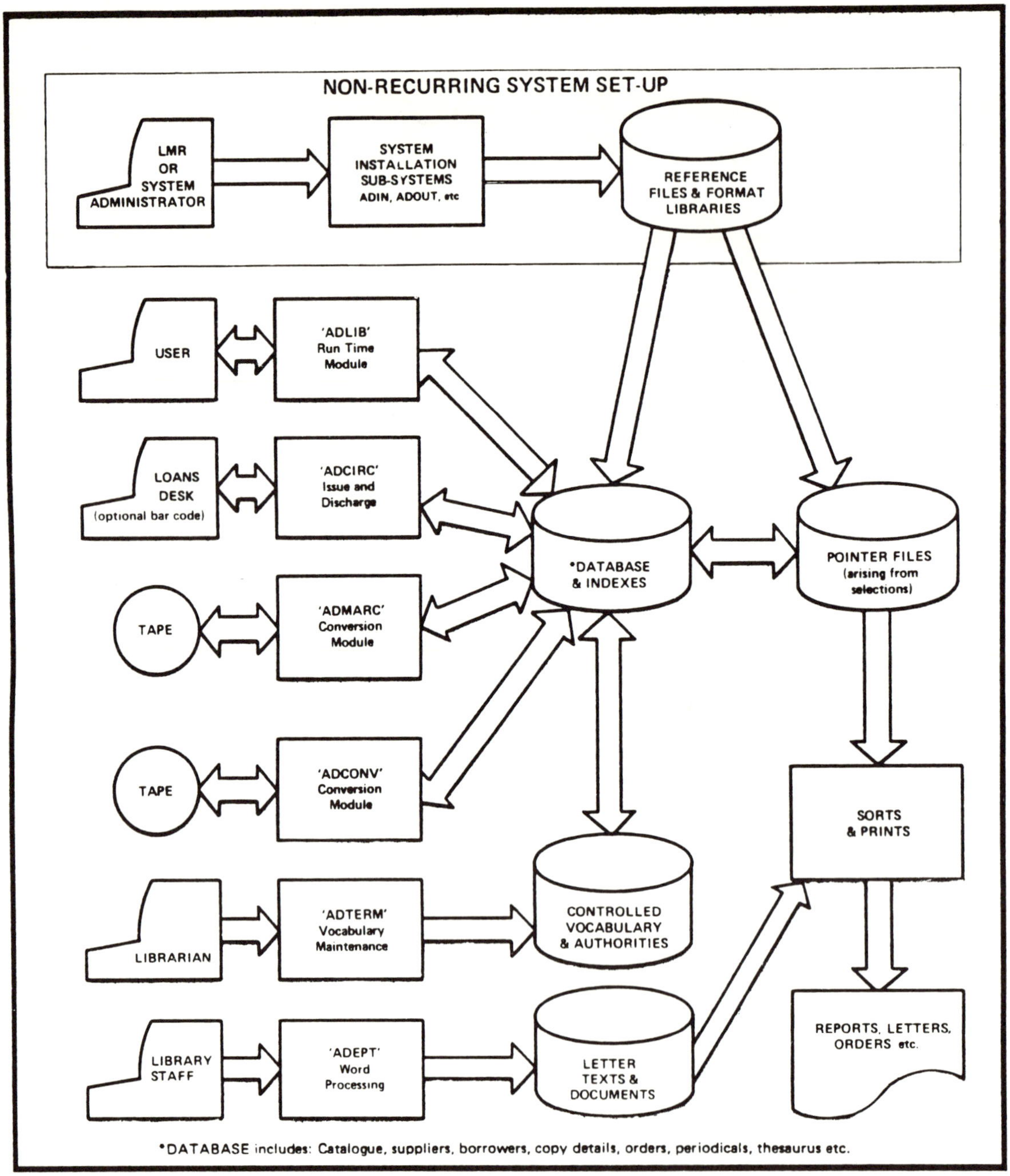

Despite rapid developments, few systems available, even today, are completely integrated with *all* subsystems and files working together, sharing a common database (although several are approaching this capability). Among the last subsystems to be included are acquisitions (although this was one of the first subsystems developed by CLSI), serials control and documents (which is usually a separate database). Substantial progress is being made, however, and significant advancements will be seen in the field within the next five years.

As always, there are risks associated with developing or adopting new automated systems, as opposed to remaining with the "old" comfortable systems. Before investing substantial sums of money in a system, librarians should be aware of the principles, options, problems and promises of integrated library systems. The balance of this book examines how to plan for, evaluate and implement an IOLS, in light of the current systems available.

FOOTNOTES

1. Edward A. Chapman, Paul L. St. Pierre and John Lubans Jr., *Library Systems Analysis Guidelines* (New York: Wiley-Interscience, John Wiley & Sons, 1970).

2. Richard De Gennaro, "Library Automation: Changing Patterns and New Directions," *Library Journal* 101 (January 1976): 175-83.

3. Richard De Gennaro, "Library Automation and Networking: Perspectives on Three Decades," *Library Journal* 108 (April 1, 1983): 629-35.

4. Emily Gallup Fayen, *The Online Catalog: Improving Public Access to Library Materials* (White Plains, NY: Knowledge Industry Publications, Inc. 1983), p. 2.

5. National Aeronautics and Space Administration, *COSMIC: A Catalog of Selected Computer Programs,* (1979), pp. 20, 23. Programs are available from the Computer Software Management and Information Center (COSMIC), 112 Barrow Hall, University of Georgia, Athens, GA 30602. Though technologically dated by now, it is significant that availability of this program was not known for several years.

6. Charles M. Goldstein and Richard S. Dick, "The Lister Hill Center Integrated Library System (ILS)," *National Library of Medicine News* 35 (1) (January 1980): 1,2.

7. Association of Research Libraries, Office of Management Studies, Systems and Procedures Exchange Center, "Integrated Library Information Systems in ARL Libraries," *Spec Flyer,* no. 90 (Washington, DC: January 1983).

8. Karl Nyren and John Berry, "Information & Technology: At the Crossroads," *Library Journal* 108 (November 1, 1983): 2021.

9. Charles M. Goldstein, Elizabeth A. Payne and Richard S. Dick, Lister Hill National Center for Biomedical Communications, "The Integrated Library System (ILS): System Overview," (Springfield, VA: National Technical Information Service, 1981). Report NLM-DF-81-003.C, NTIS report no. PB81-188039.1.

10. De Gennaro, "Library Automation and Networking," op. cit.

11. Chapman, St Pierre and Lubans Jr., op. cit.

2

Planning for an IOLS

Ultimately, satisfaction with an integrated online library system will be directly related to how thoroughly the library conducts the planning process. This chapter will review the areas that should be considered in planning for an IOLS. These include an analysis of the library's needs and resources, consideration of the options available, determining the system requirements and surveying staff attitudes. Each of these areas will be examined in detail.

NEEDS ASSESSMENT

Conducting a sophisticated needs assessment for an integrated online library system is somewhat like assessing the need for library services in an organization that does not have a library. It is difficult to adequately foretell all the library's needs, because more will undoubtedly be generated once the system is installed. Obviously, no amount of planning will eliminate every risk or foresee every change in the library's future. However, a thorough needs assessment can reduce the possibility of failure and alert the library to requirements that may surface at a later date.

Why an IOLS?

First, the library must ask why it needs an integrated online library system. Is it because the present system is chaotic and the library believes that an automated system will resolve all the problems? Because budgets are dwindling and it will save the library money? Because the library needs better control of its holdings? Because better service is needed? Because it will be easier to share resources? Let us briefly address these issues.

First, automated or integrated systems do not inherently make bad systems good. Although a well-developed system will improve processes, more important, it will force the library to examine its procedures and policies, to carefully define its parameters and address issues that may not have been questioned before. In addition to examining policies currently in place, the library will have to develop new policies as procedures are more precisely defined. If procedures have been sloppy or data input (card cataloging) is inaccurate, automation will not eliminate human error. It will, however, force clarification and improvement because mistakes suddenly become more exposed.

Although there may be eventual cost savings (filing in the catalog will not be needed, for example), the immediate task of data conversion, the need to ensure bibliographic integrity of the holdings records and the potential for adding large collections of titles that previously were not included in the card catalog should realistically temper savings estimates. Besides, the maintenance cost of an IOLS can easily be equal to several salaries. Hence, the net savings may not be as great as anticipated.

If better inventory control, greater opportunity for identifying and exchanging holdings records, and better service is your goal, purchase is much more justifiable.

Resources Available

Consider the library's resources. How much money do you have or can you realistically obtain? Next, consider the allocations. If you are purchasing software and hardware independently, software could cost 50% to 70% (depending on the size of the system) of the total price. Can other terminals or systems within the institution or jurisdiction be used? If so, a software-only package might be the least expensive alternative.

The library should also assess its physical resources. This includes determining how much space the library has, or can make available, for the IOLS and analyzing the environment that the system will be functioning in. Adequate wiring, temperature control, security and the location of any printers, terminals and the computer itself should be considered. The physical resource requirements for an IOLS are examined more closely in Chapter 4.

It is especially important to consider the level of expertise of the library staff. Do staff members have minimal computer training and experience, or are they qualified programmers? The level of staff expertise will determine how much training is necessary and may also affect the type of system chosen. The level of staff experience may also have a bearing on the amount of user resistance to the new system.

IOLS AUTOMATION OPTIONS

Once the library has examined the need for an IOLS, and has a clear idea of its available resources, it must learn what options are available. Automation has become a complex issue for libraries today. Libraries must choose from among a variety of automation options, including timesharing or resource sharing, turnkey systems, independent hardware and software purchase, and in-house development. Each of these is briefly described below. A comparison of the options follows.

Timesharing

Timesharing has been defined by Mary Coyle of MITRE Corp. as an arrangement in which an organization pays a vendor or agency for the use of the vendor's computer to store a database and for general use of the system. Typically, the computer facilities are located at the vendor's site, which is within range of a local telephone call. The vendor maintains the facility and the organization rents computer time, storage space and equipment from the vendor.[1]

These are the essential elements of timesharing, although the types of charges may vary depending on whether or not the computer system and storage devices are owned by the library's parent organization (university, county, municipality, regional cooperative, government agency or corporation). In some instances these charges may only be "funny money"—transfers on the books without real cash changing hands.

Turnkey Systems

The turnkey system is a complete system, installed by a vendor on the library's premises. The library literally turns the key and the system runs. Actually, this is an overly simplistic statement since training in the operation of the system is still required. Usually the vendor is a for-profit company and is responsible for dealing with any problems of both hardware and software. There is no one else to blame if the system goes down, and problems cannot readily be shunted from hardware to software service.

Independent Purchase

Software and hardware can be purchased independently or cooperatively from other (non-turnkey) vendors. Software-only vendors are typically universities, although some software packages are available from vendors such as Battelle and BRS. It must be remembered that software is not universal to all brands of hardware and is designed to run, or run best, on the hardware that it was developed on. Software vendors will sometimes assist in defining equipment configurations for a particular installation, and some will even work very closely with the hardware vendor. In fact, in some cases, the quotation will come from the hardware vendor for both software and hardware.

When software and hardware are purchased independently, maintenance problems can arise, since the complex interdependence of software and hardware makes identification of the source of a problem difficult. In an extreme case, the hardware vendor could say that the problem is software related, while the software vendor could insist it is a hardware problem. To complicate matters even further, they could both be right and there could be a cause and effect relationship.

In-house Development

Instead of purchasing a turnkey system or independently buying software and hardware, the library could develop its own integrated online library system in-house. Before the advent of vendors of automated systems, this was the only way to obtain a system.

With an ever-increasing number of systems available for purchase, in-house development has been declining. However, some libraries are beginning to develop modules using utility packages within the newer operating systems. These utility packages, called database management systems (DBMS), contain preprogrammed operations. For example, previously the computer had to be told how to sort or file with a detailed program. With a DBMS, the computer can be told to sort, file or create a template with separate fields, and retrieve any one of them in alphabetical order, with a one word command.

As these packages become more fully developed for libraries there may be a resurgence of local system development.

COMPARING AUTOMATION OPTIONS

There are various guidelines for comparing automation options which libraries can use in planning for an IOLS. A number of these are discussed below.

Timesharing vs. Stand-alone Systems

Cost Considerations

Should a stand-alone, independent turnkey system be purchased or should a timeshared system, dependent on the computer system of the parent institution or other agency in the community, be considered? Mary Coyle analyzed the costs of these systems over time. She applied cost amortization of the turnkey installation costs and timesharing environment costs over a five-year period and concluded that, with some qualifications, "it will be more expensive to timeshare as you reach and exceed five years, but the short run may be cheaper and safer, especially if you do not want to commit your organizaiton to a system indefinitely."[2]

Coyle further cites some of the advantages of timesharing as lower initial cost, minimization of hardware problems, speedier implementation and ease of entering into a self-contained environment. The chief disadvantage is limited control over system development and operation.[3]

An article in *Library Systems Newsletter* cites a brief formula for determining which arrangement to select. It notes the fixed cost of acquiring a system and relates decision making to interlibrary loan. The following formula is used to determine the cost-effectiveness of regional resource sharing.

First, calculate the five-year costs of both the "best" shared system configuration and multiple stand-alone systems. Shared configuration may cost more, primarily owing to telecommunications equipment costs and line charges. Next, make a generous but realistic projection of the total number of interlibrary loans for the same five-year period. (Experience indicates that the number of interlibrary loans doubles when libraries share a system.)

Divide the difference in cost between the shared and stand-alone configurations by the projected number of interlibrary loans for the same period to derive a cost-per-interlibrary loan differential between the two approaches.

If this cost per interlibrary loan differential is less than $1.50, the shared approach could be considered cost-effective. On the other hand, if this figure approaches $3.00 or more, it indicates that it would be wiser for the participating libraries to install multiple stand-alone systems and merely dial-up each other's systems as needed.[4]

Special Considerations for Multi-type Libraries

There are special considerations for multi-type, multi-branch and multi-jurisdictional libraries, many of which are in timesharing environments. Large consortia such as those in Cincinnati or Pasadena pose special problems. According to Pat Barkalow of the Pasadena Public Library, policies need to be developed that are mutually acceptable to all members of a multi-jurisdictional consortium. Also, all members need to be aware of each other's procedures and policies.

In a consortium environment requiring more interlibrary exchange of data, telecommunication costs, which are rising, will be greater for all participants. Software costs might be shared through a joint purchase. Also, large systems tend to get better response from vendors for software changes and enhancements because they are in a better bargaining position.[5]

In-house Development vs. Purchase

Development of an in-house system requires library staff members who are capable programmers (or access to this expertise), systems analysts and others, and a lot of time, dedication, patience and financial support from the institution. The obvious advantages are very close control over software development and customized programming uniquely adapted to the library's needs. Enhancements can be developed locally and the library can set its own priorities in developing them. The library is completely autonomous in the development and maintenance of its system. If the system is developed in a timesharing environment, instead of on its own stand-alone computer, costs can be reduced, since the library does not have to buy its own computer hardware.

The disadvantages are that in-house development requires a high degree of computer expertise among the staff. Staff does turn over and your best analysts or programmers could leave, with the result that time would be lost in retraining new staff. In addition, unless the in-house system is made user-friendly, it may require more computer knowledge of its users than they currently possess. Then, too, the necessary financial support and patience of institutional board members or supervisors may not be readily available.

Table 2.1 summarizes the advantages and disadvantages of developing an in-house system and purchasing a developed system. Some of the concepts could also be applied more generally to consideration of any system.

Table 2.1: Comparison of In-house Development vs. Purchase

In-house Development	Purchase System
Advantages	
1. System tailored to requirements.	1. System tested and proven.
2. High degree of design integration possible.	2. Implementation time reduced.
3. Optimum use of organizational resources possible.	3. Advantages/disadvantages known.
4. Advanced state-of-the-art techniques utilized.*	4. Developmental resources freed for other efforts.
	5. Usually less expensive.
Disadvantages	
1. Lengthy development time.	1. Does not meet all requirements.
2. Costs and benefits uncertain.	2. Inefficient use of resources.
3. Developmental talents are scarce and not always available.	3. Maintenance and modification are a greater problem.
4. Debugging and other problems occur long after implementation.	4. Less integration with other systems.
5. Usually more expensive.	5. Demoralizing to developmental staff.
	6. Generally, not state-of-the-art.

*State-of-the-art techniques are more apt to be employed by libraries creating customized systems than by vendors, which are primarily interested in generalizing their systems to sell to a broader base of library customers.

Source: John G. Burch, Jr., Felix R. Strater and Gary Grudnitski, *Information Systems: Theory and Practice,* 2nd ed. © 1979 (John Wiley & Sons). Reprinted with permission.

In general, in-house development is very often prohibited by the cost of the labor and the amount of expertise required. However, as noted earlier, the availability of increasingly sophisticated software combined with more powerful, less expensive computers may spur growth in this area.

Purchase Options

Assuming the library decides to purchase an IOLS, there are essentially three broad options available: transferring software from another library (installed user package), purchasing a modified turnkey system or purchasing a complete turnkey system. Table 2.2 depicts these options along with summary information on each. Keep in mind that there are many variations among these options, with some systems falling between. Therefore, Table 2.2 presents them as a continuum (Type 1, Type 3, etc.) rather than as rigidly defined categories.

Installed User Package

The installed user software package is exemplified by the IBM Dobis/Leuven system (see Chapter 6). As mentioned previously, the risk associated with purchasing software, whether from a library or a commercial vendor, is that it is difficult to place responsibility for the hardware and software running together.[6] Also, there is often little support for software other than that which can be obtained from other users, and development of programs is frequently entirely local.

Modified Turnkey System

The modified turnkey system is typified by the Virginia Tech Library System (VTLS) (see Chapter 6). It is a turnkey system that uses unmodified or off-the-shelf equipment (i.e., the equipment can still be used for other applications). The software vendor is an academic university. With a modified turnkey system, source codes are provided and program development can be shared by both library staff and the vendor.

Complete Turnkey System

In a complete turnkey system, all software is proprietary and the equipment is built by the vendor from the microchip to the outside casing. Geac (discussed in Chapter 6) is an example of this type of system. All equipment is housed in the library, which has exclusive access to it. Virtually all program development must be handled by the vendor, and the library is totally reliant upon the vendor for new subsystems or enhancements.

DETERMINING SYSTEM REQUIREMENTS

One of the most important steps in the planning process is determining the system requirements for an IOLS. In the planning stage, the library need not be concerned with developing a detailed statement of how the system will operate. Rather, the library should decide what basic functions it wants the IOLS to perform. Staff participation in this part of the planning process is essential. "Classified staff [clerical], whose jobs will be most affected, should be involved, along with professional staff . . . If they are involved in the planning for the redistribution of activities, acceptance of the system will be easier."[7]

At the very least, the library will want to be able to perform the major functions of collection acquisition and organization (cataloging), inventory control (circulation), and public access through indexing (public access catalog). As noted earlier, few integrated online library systems have all subsystems available. Therefore, the library staff should decide on some priorities in the planning stage regarding which subsystems they must have immediately and which modules they are willing to wait for, or, in some cases, forego.

Table 2.2: Comparison of Purchase Options

	Type 1: Installed User Package	Type 3: Modified Turnkey System	Type 5: Complete Turnkey System
Description	Software package that runs on existing library equipment.	Independently purchased software and hardware.	Hardware and software interdependent and must be purchased together.
Characteristics	Computer and disk drives housed within or outside the library.	Computer and disk drives housed in the library.	Computer and disk drives housed in the library.
	Total reliance on library/computer staff for all software enhancements or modifications. No outside help for program development.	Shared program development with vendor.	Virtually total reliance on vendor for all software enhancements or modifications.
	Compatibility of library and other local records assured.	Source codes made available that would facilitate interfacing library and other local records. Compatibility easily developed.	Interfacing of library and other local records may not be possible.
Advantages	Maximum interfacing with other local records, such as bursar, voter registration, etc.	Some interfacing with other local records.	Minimum interfacing with other local records.

Table 2.2: Comparison of Purchase Options (Cont.)

	Type 1: Installed User Package	Type 3: Modified Turnkey System	Type 5: Complete Turnkey System
Advantages (cont'd.)	Maximum number of terminals could be purchased, since existing computer equipment would be used. Local control of development.	Modest number of terminals could be obtained, since computer equipment would also be purchased. Shared control of development. Recent state-of-the-art. Modest impact on the library. Exclusive access to computer.	Modest number of terminals could be obtained, since computer equipment would also be purchased. Outside control of development. Recent state-of-the-art. Minimal impact on the library. Exclusive access to computer.
Disadvantages	Earlier technology. Library workload could significantly increase. Shared access to computer. Total reliance on library or computer center staff to develop software programs.	Some reliance upon library staff for interfacing records.	Total reliance on vendor for all software, including interfacing.

In addition, the library staff should develop a list of the functions needed within each subsystem; for example, the library may want the circulation subsystem to permit online check-in, online renewals, etc. Specific functions such as these can be found in the vendor survey (see Appendix A). Although each library's specific requirements will vary, the survey list can serve as a starting point.

Both in terms of the subsystems and specific functions, the library staff should develop a list of absolutely necessary items, i.e., those performed by the present system, whether manual or automated; a list of items needed but not available; and a list of desired items. This weighting of specifications will aid in the later evaluation and selection process.

In addition, the library should determine the size of patron and title files, since the total number of records will, in part, determine the size of the system, hardware requirements and the amount of disk space needed.

STAFF ATTITUDES

Determining staff attitudes toward administrative issues connected with the selection of an integrated online library system is as important as choosing the right hardware and software. Staff attitudes will further govern the choice between in-house, turnkey or mixed system. Bear in mind that none of these options is necessarily good or bad, recommended or not recommended. What must be determined is how library staff members react to the basic administrative issues involved.

A very conspicuous issue is the degree of reliance the library is willing to place on outside sources for development. Some librarians prefer the opportunity to develop a program from the ground up, and to be heavily involved in the actual programming of the system. Others prefer the hands-off approach and wish to leave all computer programming and analysis to outside help.

Other issues are: library autonomy versus dependence on outside vendors; interfacing capabilities between library files and the parent organization; timeshared versus exclusive access to computer equipment; and direct contact with maintenance personnel as compared with contact through an intermediary.

At Youngstown State University (YSU) a survey instrument was developed to determine the attitudes of staff and patrons toward these and other issues. A 14-member task force, including professional librarians, clerical personnel, a student representative and a faculty representative, was surveyed.

The survey (see Figure 2.1) was divided into three main sections. The first section dealt with preferences regarding equipment, software, interfacing, maintenance and, finally, the system as a whole. The second section was designed to determine staff attitudes toward tradeoffs. This section was devised to ascertain what features the staff would be willing to give up in order to acquire a given system. In the third section, respondents were

(Text continues on page 29)

Figure 2.1: Youngstown State University Library Survey of Attitudes Toward IOLS

Since it will not be possible to view all integrated library systems nor will it be feasible to study them to the depth that is needed, your attitudes regarding some of the managerial issues that override decisions governing the choice of a system are desired. These issues can be depicted on a continuum. There are a wide range of options available for an integrated library system. If a line were drawn from left to right in a continuum, one option or type would be on the extreme left and the opposite type would be on the extreme right, with a progressive number of options in between the extremes. The Chart of Options depicts the types of options available. Bear in mind that MORE than the three types depicted are available; but only three have been provided in order to conserve space. These systems represent everything from a low-cost, "do-it-yourself" type system with older software and technology to a higher-cost system, using the latest computer technology, with virtually everything done for you. Each reflects varying degrees of autonomy and independence in software development and maintenance support. Study this chart and then answer the questions in this survey form. Remember, you are not voting for a single system at this time. You are ONLY being asked to express your opinion regarding administrative issues reflected in the various systems.

Purpose:

To survey the Computer Library Systems Task Force regarding attitudes toward administrative issues governing the selection of an automated library system.

Definitions:

Type--Refers to a set of characteristics, advantages and disadvantages that represent an option. There are several more "types" or options than are depicted in the chart. Some of these fall between Type 1 and Type 3 or between Type 3 and Type 5. That is why the numbers 1 to 5 have been given underneath each continuum, in order for you to express an opinion that falls between these types.

Figure 2.1 (Cont.)

SECTION I: PREFERENCES

In the questions that follow, think of each concept as having two extremes with a progressive shift from the one on the left to the one on the right.

Please circle the number representing the place in the continuum that you feel would be the best option for the Library to follow in the selection of an automated system.

1. EQUIPMENT PREFERENCE--HARDWARE (circle choice)

   ```
   .................................................
   1           2           3           4           5
   ```

   ALL computer equipment housed in the Computer Center. No computer disks or tape drive in the Library. Terminals only in the Library. Access shared with all other components of University.

   ALL computer equipment under Library control, housed in Library, and independent or stand-alone. Exclusive access to computer.

2. SOFTWARE PREFERENCE (circle choice)

   ```
   .................................................
   1           2           3           4           5
   ```

   TOTAL reliance on Library and Computer Center staff to develop all program enhancements and modifications.

   TOTAL reliance on outside vendor to develop all program enhancements and modifications.

3. INTERFACING (circle choice)

   ```
   .................................................
   1           2           3           4           5
   ```

   Maximum compatibility and interchangeability of Library and YSU (Bursar, Registrar) records.

   Minimum compatibility and interchangeability of Library and YSU (Bursar, Registrar) records.

Figure 2.1 (Cont.)

4. SERVICE MAINTENANCE (circle choice)

   ....
   1   2   3   4   5

   Indirect control over   Maximum contact with ser-
   equipment service, i.e.   vice representative.
   through the Computer Cen-
   ter. Minimum contact
   with service representative.

5. SYSTEM PREFERENCE AS A WHOLE. Refer to the Chart of Options and indicate the type that is most in agreement with your preferences. Circle one number only.

   ....
   1   2   3   4   5

   Type 1.   Type 3.   Type 5.
   Installed User   Modified Turnkey   Complete Turnkey
   Package   System   System

6. OTHER (specify) _____ (circle choice)

   ....
   1   2   3   4   5

   _____
   _____
   _____

SECTION II: TRADEOFFS

This section is designed to determine items that you would be willing to give up in order to obtain your preferences as indicated above, especially where there is a conflict.

Check yes or no under each.   YES   NO

7. TECHNOLOGY. I would be willing to trade the newer state-of-the-art (1980's) technology   _____   _____
   and software for older (1970's) technology to obtain my preference.

Figure 2.1 (Cont.)

8. SERVICE. I would trade fast hardware/software service for slower hardware/software service to obtain my preferences.

    YES ____ NO ____

9. DEVELOPMENT. I would be willing to trade a system with several acceptable, operational subsystems, such as acquisitions, on-line catalog, etc., for a system with a single, outstanding subsystem that I prefer, such as an on-line catalog, assuming that other subsystems were to be made available in the future.

    YES ____ NO ____

10. OTHER TRADEOFFS. (Specify) _____

SECTION III: RANKINGS

List what you consider to be the five most important issues in selecting an automated library system in rank order. Most important at the top. Least important at the bottom.

1. _____
2. _____
3. _____
4. _____
5. _____

SECTION IV: ADDITIONAL COMMENTS

_____
_____
_____

THANK YOU FOR YOUR COOPERATION.

_____
(signature)

(Text continued from page 24)
asked to rank the most important considerations in obtaining an integrated system in an open-ended, free-form list.

The majority of the respondents indicated a desire to have close control of the system, with a basic developed turnkey system that was modifiable. Most respondents wanted direct maximum contact with service representatives. The majority would also sacrifice minute differences in response time in order to obtain other desired features. In the rankings question, the most important issue was system reliability. Quick efficient service ranked next, followed by a sufficient number of terminals. Immediate availability of all subsystems, as opposed to waiting for various subsystems to develop, was ranked fourth. Demonstrated success of the system, compatibility with present records, a training program and OCLC/MARC format were other desired features.

What is important in the planning process is not the specific results of this survey, or even the survey form itself. The reader may devise a better one. Most important is the concept of involving staff members and discovering their attitudes toward the overall issues. When specifics are considered, these overall attitudes will help narrow the field and guide the administrator's selection of a system. In addition, staff will have had a part in the selection process and will have been made aware of some of the broader issues.

A staff survey should help resolve such questions as whether to get one system, which has an excellent online public access catalog but does not have an acquisition system fully developed, or another, which has several subsystems developed and available. It can help you decide whether to concentrate on, for instance, turnkey systems or the modifiable systems. More important, in addition to narrowing the field choices, adherence to staff responses will provide a feeling of involvement and ultimately, a better climate of acceptance.

SUMMARY

Good planning is a time-consuming, often costly, undertaking. However, it is the basis for careful and meaningful evaluation and, therefore, worth the library's investment. Many of the considerations in planning for a system are the very items that will be used in the evaluation of a system, the subject of Chapter 3.

FOOTNOTES

1. Mary L. Coyle, "The Integrated Library in a Timesharing Evironment," in *Conference on Integrated Online Library Systems, September 26-27, 1983: Proceedings,* rev. ed. (Canfield, OH: Genaway & Associates, Inc., 1984).

2. Coyle, op. cit.

3. Coyle, op. cit.

4. "Stand-alone or Shared? Costings and Considerations in Turnkey Configurations," *Library Systems Newsletter* 3(4) (April 1983): 25-27.

5. Pat Barkalow, "Impact of IOLS on Multi-Jurisdictional Libraries in Consortia," in *Conference on Integrated Online Library Systems, September 26-27, 1983: Proceedings,* rev. ed. (Canfield, OH: Genaway & Associates, Inc., 1984).

6. Richard W. Boss, *The Library Manager's Guide to Automation, 2nd edition* (White Plains, New York: Knowledge Industry Publications, Inc., 1984).

7. David C. Genaway, "Selecting an Integrated Online Library System: Attitudes Toward Administrative Issues" (unpublished manuscript), p. 3.

3

System Evaluation and Selection

In order to evaluate systems, the library must have some guidelines and criteria for comparison. We will assume that suggestions made in Chapter 2 have been followed: i.e., that the assessment of the library's resources has been made, the alternatives available have been considered, the system requirements have been defined and a survey of staff attitudes toward the administrative issues has been conducted.

This chapter will review various methods of obtaining information on integrated systems as a prelude to evaluation and selection. It offers several guidelines for evaluating integrated systems along with specific selection criteria. In addition, the trade-offs inherent in the IOLS selection process are discussed. This chapter will also report on a survey of IOLS users, conducted for this book.

OBTAINING INFORMATION

The process of collecting information on integrated systems begins when the library starts to investigate the various options available, if not before. However, library staff members need to have their knowledge of integrated systems developed to the point where they can contribute to the evaluation and selection of a system. The more knowledgeable the staff becomes, the more intelligent the decision will be. Literature reviews and on-site, demonstrations are two ways of obtaining information on systems, prior to the more formal procedures of issuing specifications, requests for proposals (RFPs) and requests for quotations (RFQs).

While it may be desirable to have everyone who will be affected by the IOLS involved in the evaluation process, this is not always feasible. One institution, the University of Missouri, did involve its entire library staff and users in the information gathering and subsequent evaluation process. More than 1000 persons attended one of hundreds of demonstrations of online and COM catalogs over a six-week period.[1] The more common approach is to form a task force consisting of library staff members and users. The task force will be instrumental in collecting information and can also be used to survey vendors and users of integrated systems. It will not always be possible to study every system to the degree of depth desired, but the task force approach will allow considerable involvement by many well-informed staff.

Literature Review

This should include identification and review of articles, books and news releases about systems, as well as literature from the various vendors. A file of such information can be circulated to task force members.

In general, articles will tend to be more objective than evaluative. When reading ads or corporate literature, look not so much for features advertised as for omissions. What features were not advertised that you are concerned about? Compare advertisements. By so doing you learn what points to look for.

Literature evaluating software is somewhat difficult to find; however, this may change as the trend toward providing software reviews in journals continues. Evaluations of hardware can be found in the publications put out by Auerbach and Datapro, and from scanning computer magazines such as *Computerworld*. (Citations for these and other resources are given in the bibliography at the end of this book.)

On-site Demonstrations

There are few substitutes for hands-on experience. Therefore, on-site demonstrations, where staff members can see the system in action and question the vendor about specific capabilities, are valuable. Following some simple guidelines for demonstrations will help make them more successful.

First, staff should have substantial information about each system, prior to the demonstration, in order to make it more meaningful. Data should be gathered well in advance and circulated to staff. Folders or packets can be compiled and placed on reserve or checked out from the director's office. Thus, the director will know whether staff members have done their homework.

Demonstrations usually take one or two days; therefore, it is best if some kind of schedule is drawn up. A certain time period should be allotted for demonstration of each subsystem: serials, acquisitions, etc. Staff from these sections can then come prepared with a list of questions gleaned from their readings. Throughout the day there should be periods designated for the demonstration of the online catalog subsystem, which will be most useful to the general user. It is sometimes easier to attract vendors if they know that other library heads or staff members are being invited to these demonstrations, particularly if your library is a small- or medium-sized one.

Provide the vendor with appropriate maps of the city and/or library area. Make provisions for receiving and storing equipment, and designate a specific area for the demonstration. Make sure that there is a "clean" outside telephone line nearby, adequate electrical outlets and, if possible, an extra monitor for larger audiences.

Let the vendor know in advance what type of equipment and setup will be available. Also, assist the vendor with directions for sending equipment back. First of all, you want a smooth demonstration; second, you, too, are establishing a relationship with the vendor. Vendors do have a considerable expense associated with on-site demonstrations and, ultimately, only one can be awarded the contract.

Evaluation sheets with stated criteria might be distributed to all staff prior to the demonstration. This will also help assure uniformity and objectivity in evaluating presentations. A post-mortem of each demonstration can be conducted immediately afterward to compare data.

RFIs, RFPs and RFQs

There are three more formal ways of obtaining information about a particular system from a vendor: the request or call for information (RFI or CFI), the request for proposal (RFP) and the request for quotation (RFQ). The RFI or CFI seeks to determine basic product information and determine potential eligibility of the vendor. The RFP provides information about the library to the vendor, identifies specific system requirements and asks the vendor to address these items by proposing a system that will meet these needs. The RFQ is usually accompanied by specifications with a suggested configuration. When issuing an RFQ, a library states exactly what it wants and the parameters necessary, and the vendor provides a quotation, representing a formal bid.

The logical sequence, though not necessarily a rigidly followed one, is to issue a call for information first. If the whole process were to be followed in sequence, the call for information would be issued, followed by an RFP, followed by an RFQ or actual bid. In actuality, if all three steps are followed to the letter, there is an enormous amount of paperwork and considerable redundancy.

Another word of caution is in order. Just as libraries spend a considerable amount of time identifying their needs and articulating them in a proposal, the vendor spends a considerable amount of time responding. The difference is that the vendor is committed to proposal statements and can lose a lot of money if estimates are miscalculated. Hence, do not send such requests or proposals to vendors if there is no serious interest and a reasonable assurance that purchase funds are available.

Vendor Survey

As the pool of RFPs and RFQs available for study becomes larger, each library tends to copy all the best parts from previous RFPs, in addition to adding its own improvements and embellishments. The resulting document can be very difficult for a vendor to respond to accurately. As an alternative, the library can precisely identify the subsystems and requirements that are absolutely essential, and develop an RFI that can be answered quickly. (The vendor survey form shown in Appendix A can be used for this purpose.*) Then, the library can eliminate vendors that do not match the basic requirements and request specific bids from those remaining.

Probably the most important information the library must obtain in a vendor survey is the operational status of the various IOLS subsystems. The survey findings presented in Appendix A can serve as a guide, and represent a snapshot of the industry as of April 1984. However, the industry is a motion picture, and any library acquiring an IOLS should update the information given in the Appendix by conducting its own survey.†

User Survey

It is important, where possible, to visit other libraries where a particular system is installed. In addition, staff should attend conferences whenever possible and query colleagues at every opportunity. The advantages of a conference are that there are usually a number of experts in attendance, along with a wide variety of practitioners, and side-by-side exhibits that can be compared.

To augment site visits—or instead of them, where such visits are not possible—members of the task force can be assigned to survey users of the system by telephone, possibly contacting persons they know at libraries where the system is used. Findings can be reported to the group. A survey form should be used when calling users to obtain evaluations of systems. As in the case of evaluating demonstrations, a standard questionnaire will assure a more uniform basis for comparing answers. The form should, however, allow for open-ended or additional responses.

Figure 3.1 reproduces the survey form used to obtain evaluations for Youngstown State University. Obviously, the key factors to be determined are reliability, serviceability, satisfaction and problems. Keep in mind that not all problems are insurmountable or unbearable. There will be problems associated with every system. The virtues of any system are also most likely to be its detriments. Two systems, for example, may be equally fast in finding 40 records by a given author or subject heading, but one system may appear to have a faster response time than the other. However, the one with the "faster" response

---

*Ellen Miller, director of library systems development at the University of Cincinnati Libraries, has also outlined the basic elements of a CFI. The table of contents for the Greater Cincinnati Library Consortium CFI is an excellent list of the kinds of information that should be provided to vendors and solicited from them. Basic plans with statistical data should be provided to the vendor, in addition to a description of activities, the type of system sought, management reports required, any constraints on the software and the hardware needed. Maintenance, documentation, training, installation plan, pre-installation assistance and basic business information are called for.[2]

†The May 1, 1984 issue of *Library Journal* also contains an excellent summary and overview of the industry.[3]

time may present the records in random order while the one with the "slower" response time presents all the records in sorted order.

Also, be sure to take into account any extenuating circumstances when calling for an evaluation of a system. For example, at least one university has its own repair technicians. Hence, its downtime, or field service response time, may be significantly different from that in your library, which does not have such a luxury.

Is the installation being contacted a test site for that system? If so, it is likely to have received favored treatment. Does the system operate with multiprocessors? If so, its 100% up-time may be accounted for by the fact that it can switch from one processor to another, if necessary. The age of a particular system, the local environment it is operating in and any problems that may have negatively affected its operation are other issues to consider.

GUIDELINES FOR EVALUATION

In order to put the information gathered on integrated systems to use in actually selecting an IOLS, the library must establish some guidelines for evaluation. Otherwise, the library will find itself awash in a sea of data, no closer to making a choice than when the process began. Following are the main points and areas of evaluation to consider.

Library Resources

The library's present human, capital and operating fiscal resources will figure heavily in the evaluation process. The degree of computer expertise among the staff will in part govern the type of system and the amount of local development anticipated. With little or no staff competency in programming or systems analysis, selection should probably be limited to turnkey systems. If the staff has computer experience, then a wider variety of systems can be considered.

Staff expertise will also have a bearing on anticipated applications. Are there well-qualified programmers on the library staff? If modifications to the program are anticipated in order to establish connections with local institutional files or databases, it is essential that such staff be available. Also, what source codes or programs must be provided by the vendor? If, on the other hand, staff expertise is limited and little or no local modification of the program is desired or intended, then access to source codes and local adaptation is not as important.

If the library has access to a large mainframe computer or several microcomputers, there should be some effort to select software and/or hardware that is compatible and can reduce overall costs of the system. The system should also be considered in relation to how effectively present resources can be used, in terms of linkages between any parent organization's computer system. If the municipality has two-way cable, or the institution already has a large number of terminals, a substantial amount of money can be saved by connecting to the library's system. The amount of money available or likely to be available is an obvious constraint that will eliminate some systems. However, as discussed later in this chapter, costs should be compared very carefully.

Functions Required

The ancients warned, "Know thyself." If the library has done a thorough job of its needs assessment during the planning stage, both staff and management will have a clear idea of all the operations of their current system, whether manual or automated.

When evaluating different IOLS alternatives, note which operations are foreground and which are background. For example, must the system be completely occupied—excluding online public access to the database and circulation transactions—while MARC tapes are being loaded or self-maintenance is being conducted? If all other operations must be shut down to conduct a specific operation, it is a foreground not a background operation. Can background operations be conducted simultaneously while the system is fully operational in all its modules or subsystems?

Consider all reports generated, management statistics, types of files and characteristics of records and files under the present system; what kinds of management reports does the IOLS make available? Are circulation statistics available by subject or patron category? Are there reports on terminal activity? Acquistions fund reports? As administrators know, statistics can be used to measure the effectiveness of the system as well as its usefulness. Management statistics, such as collection use, growth, etc., seem to be a little slow in materializing. At least one exception is the IOLS offered by CL Systems, Inc. (CLSI), which provides excellent circulation statistics with its SCAT number analysis. This creates a printout of circulation activity for each defined subject category you select, based on LC call number.

It is important to note all of the different ways in which files are accessed and data are retrieved. Ask which of these capabilities will have to be sacrificed if a particular system is acquired. You may find that several of these capabilities—taken for granted under the old system—are lacking in the system being considered. Be sure that these items are identified and anticipated *before* purchasing the system, rather than afterward.

It is easy to make assumptions about a system that may or may not be true. The safest rule is, "Assume nothing!" If the functions that you want are not explicitly stated to be available in advertising and vendor literature, you can be reasonably sure that the items are not available. The best course is to question the vendor closely on all areas of the system, checking not only on availability but operational status.

The basic principles outlined in Chapter 1 should serve as a guide in evaluating and narrowing down the choices. Remember that the basic functions of circulation, online public access, accounting, control and routing should be served. Also, consider online access to files and interchangeable files via several subsystems that are easy to use, standardized, etc.

System Origin

The library should consider its own background and type in relation to the background of the system being evaluated. For example, if an academic library is looking at a system developed in the corporate world by and for special libraries, it should examine very closely every function currently used and compare these to the functions operational and available in the system sought.

More specifically, if a system was originally developed to handle multi-media, or had its origins in a library serving the blind or visually handicapped (such as the system offered by Data Research Associates), handling of this type of material would obviously be more developed than in a system that had its origins in another type of library. This is especially important if your library is similar in nature, since the strong points you are looking for will more likely be found. Systems with their origins in medical libraries will have characteristics and features that will be most useful to other medical libraries; the same is true with public library oriented systems.

The awareness of the differences in system origins will help identify potential problems. However, this is not to say that a system cannot cross over to be valuable to a wide variety of libraries. There may be features or modules used in libraries different from your own that are valuable and desired. Also, systems are usually quite dynamic and responsive to the marketplace and their users. Features that were not available six, even two, months ago may be available now.

For example, Avatar, which grew out of the NLM system where fines were not as important as they are in academic and public libraries, initially did not have a fine procedure. This was developed in 1983, however. Similarly, in-string and truncated searches were not widely available in the early 1980s, but most systems are now making truncated and/or Boolean operator searches available. Most are also developing, or have developed, authority files. On the whole, there appears to be a growing trend toward commonality of services and subsystems available.

Terminal Access Requirements

Be sure to consider the number of terminals to be acquired in your evaluation. The optimum number of terminals per library system has not yet been established, although one per 65 or 100 students has been suggested for academic libraries. Someone has jokingly said that the number of terminals needed is like the amount of sleep the average person needs: five minutes more, or five terminals more. Public libraries should take into account the potential for catalog phone access, which takes advantage of the patron's own computer equipment.

In determining the number of terminals needed, several levels of service should be considered. For example, level one might be the basic level of service. This would be the minimal system, with all the software and hardware to build the database and provide for the operation of a single subsystem. Level two would be enough terminals for the operation of several subsystems. Level three would provide enough terminals to operate several subsystems and give online access to the library's holdings.*

The number of terminals a system can support depends on how many "ports" the CPU can support. Normally, about four terminals can be accommodated by one port. Be sure to consider the maximum number of ports the computer system being evaluated can support without being upgraded. If the maximum is not considered at the outset, a new computer with more capacity may have to be purchased far sooner than you wish, just to handle additional terminals.

Data Conversion

Data conversion may be made easier or more difficult, depending on the system used: for example, some systems may load data more slowly than others. Therefore, the ease of data conversion should also be a part of the evaluation process, since it can constitute a major cost and/or a logistical problem. Data conversion must be considered from a number of perspectives. The first is converting from a manual to an automated system. The second is converting from one automated system to another.

In one sense, converting manual files to automated files might be easier. Obviously, each record could be manually input, but this is a long, slow process. In either case, it would be desirable to let a service, such as Autographics, Mini-MARC or REMARC, do most of the conversion. Transferring a set of machine-readable files from one vendor to another might be quite difficult, especially if cooperation of the outgoing vendor is required. If the MARC archive tapes have been saved this might be the best route. With the cooperation of both the outgoing vendor, the incoming vendor and/or local computer staff, it may be possible to bridge the two databases. Yet another alternative is to use a large computer at the hardware vendor's site to create a disk of converted records that can be readily mounted on the same equipment when it is ready for operation at your site.

The options and methods are important when you are considering switching vendors. Data conversion from abbreviated record to full bibliographic record is likely to be easiest if one merely upgrades the present system with the same vendor. At least that vendor is familiar with the record format and database structure and probably has utility programs to accomplish the conversion.

Although it may seem too early for a third perspective, serious consideration should be given to the ease with which data can be transferred when the new system being acquired is replaced. At the 1983 Library and Information Technology Association (LITA) Conference, panelists on integrated systems felt that the most important aspect of an inte-

---

*It is important to note that although there is a shift in activities at this level of service (e.g., no filing in the public catalog) it is not wise to promise staff reductions. Instead, one might control the rising staff needs. It is somewhat ironic that additional computerization automatically increases the staff needs of a computer center, but if any other area is computerized, the administration frequently expects staff reductions.

grated system was the database, because the machines will be replaced at the end of that commonly accepted "inexorable" seven year cycle.[4]

One of the concepts that librarians must adjust to is the changing lifecycle of library operations. Computer systems are estimated to have a standard life of five to seven years at which point they will be either outdated by new technology that can perform more functions at a faster rate and provide even more services, or the equipment just becomes old and begins to malfunction. Just as the concept of weeding has always been somewhat alien to librarians, as opposed to the concepts of conservation, preservation and permanency, librarians will have to adjust to a less tangible product as records are placed on disks instead of those touchable cards that one can readily identify as having filed or typed. Computer records seem less permanent than the eternal card catalog. After all, the card catalog represents a great deal of very visible work, contributed over the years. Now, that work will no longer be as visible, and will be less permanent than the card catalog.

The idea of changing a whole system and reloading the database every five to seven years will take some time to adjust to, but it must be considered, nonetheless. In evaluating the current system, consideration must be given to the ease of upgrading or making a transition to another system in the future.

Vendor Background and Reliability

The vendor's background, experience and track record are most important. Consider the history and background of the corporation and/or institution. Note the background of the chief officers and the type of experience the vendor has had. Available corporate reports should be studied to determine whether the company is growing or declining.

Reliability (how often does the system need service?) and maintenance (how quickly and how well is it serviced?) are key factors of evaluation. It is better to have a system that lacks some of the features the library wants but is up all the time, than to have a complete system that is continually breaking down. As noted earlier, it is best to check published reports on hardware and to talk to users of the system to determine the degree of reliability and the quality of service. The results of the IOLS user survey, summarized at the end of this chapter, will provide some broad perspectives on these issues.

COMPARING COSTS

Determining actual or accurate costs for an IOLS is frequently tricky. First, it is difficult to get comparable cost estimates. Some vendors will want to quote the total price of the system, including every feature the library could ever need. At first, such a quotation may appear high. However, when compared with the base price for the actual software and equipment offered by other vendors, the price may actually be lower.

Just as some supermarkets are willing to lose money on "loss leaders" because they can make it up on other items that are sold with the loss leaders, some vendors operate similarly. For example, turnkey vendors sometimes rely on higher equipment prices while software may be relatively inexpensive. Carefully check the quoted prices for terminals, disks, computers and peripherals and compare them with standard prices found in Auerbach or Datapro guides. In one case, the standard price of terminals was $600 less than the $1200 quoted by the vendor. If a library finds itself in this situation, but likes the system, it can ask to purchase the terminals independently. However, keep in mind that if terminals are purchased separately, the library will have to make its own arrangements for maintenance. This may defeat part of the purpose for going with a turnkey vendor in the first place.

A software-only vendor, of course, makes its money solely from the sale of the software. Thus, the price may not be as negotiable and the cost of the software will be relatively high-priced when compared with the turnkey vendor's quote. However, keep in mind that the equipment is likely to be purchased at dealer cost. If your library is the first in the state or region to consider a particular system, or you can arrange a joint or multiple installation (as was the case in West Virginia), you may be in a better position to bargain.

In all cost analysis be sure that you are comparing similar equipment capabilities, mass storage, etc., as much as possible. One way to do this is to arbitrarily state several levels of operation and obtain a price for each. For example, the system must be capable of storing 400,000 titles and 30,000 patron records and provide support for 10 terminals at one level, 20 terminals at another level, etc. This example is an oversimplification, but it should convey the idea.

Keep in mind that adding one to four terminals to the system or changing the database size could mean that a much more powerful and more expensive computer might be needed. Make sure that the vendor has quoted an adequate amount of equipment to handle your present capacity, plus growth for at least five years. It is not a pleasant surprise to find that you have already outgrown your system, even as it is being installed.

When evaluating maintenance costs, consider the amount of coverage included. There may be a difference in maintenance costs based on the desired service response time. For example, 24-hour service, seven days a week will cost considerably more than 8:00 a.m. to 5:00 p.m. service five days a week. Also, does the vendor incur penalties for nonfulfillment (downtime)? If so, are the penalties usually prorated, e.g., 5% reduction in maintenance contract for 5% downtime, 10% for 10% downtime, etc.?

Look very closely at the annual maintenance costs in relation to the total cost of the system and the library's total operating budget. Some vendors may have a lower initial cost but a maintenance cost that would equal the price of the total system in five years. Be sure to consider the annual maintenance in compiling future budgets. Some systems pay all transportation costs for field service representatives and include all replacement parts as part of the service agreement. Others may charge for parts or travel for the repairman. Also, determine whether replacement parts are new or used parts.

OTHER EVALUATION CRITERIA

In addition to the major areas discussed above, the following are some important points to investigate when evaluating and selecting an IOLS:

• Make sure that the source codes (i.e., the program itself) if not available, can be put in escrow, in case the firm ceases to do business. Some systems do not make the source codes available.

• Make sure that the system is upgradable or capable of expansion without requiring a totally new software package, and that it is compatible with standard telecommunications protocols. Adherence to standards facilitates compatibility and resource sharing.*

• Check if there are several levels of security. Can security be controlled by terminal location as well as level of authorization such as the ability to modify records, delete records, etc.? Is there backup for the files? How is this backup maintained? Is it on disks, tapes, computer output microfiche?

• Make sure you see the operator's manuals. These provide the most information about a system's actual capabilities and usually include sample reports. Also, they will give an indication of how easy or difficult it is to operate the system.

• Find out what kinds of supplies will be needed. Tractor feed printers for fine notices? Unique labels? Can existing labels be used if converting from one bar-coded system to another or will all labels have to be replaced?

• Find out how the system interfaces with utilities. Must a separate subsystem be purchased to accomplish the connection? Or does it merely pick up the data through the printer port of the utility terminal?

• Find out if training will be included at the vendor's site or at the installation site. Systems that market only software may have two separate training sessions, one by the software vendor and one by the equipment manufacturer. Is the training cost included in the quotation? Are all travel costs for instructors included?

---

*John Blair at the Northeastern Ohio Universities College of Medicine (Rootstown, OH) is working on a new concept in system development. Working with the Unix operating system, he is using standard operating system packages or DBMS software (rather than writing original programming) to develop an IOLS. Programming is minimal and the use of built-in routines facilitates the transportability of the program to other computers. Thus, the system is less hardware-specific.

MAKING THE FINAL SELECTION

The process of system evaluation is also a process of elimination. First, all systems not meeting the basic requirements established by the library will be eliminated. Financial constraints may further reduce the number of systems realistically available.

Rating the Systems

One way of obtaining assistance in the final selection is to have staff members rate the systems as a whole. They should list the advantages and disadvantages of each system finalist. They should be instructed to have at least one advantage and disadvantage for each system, so as to force them to think of pros and cons in case they are prejudiced for or against a given system. Staff members should then list the system they prefer and state why they would choose this system. It should be clear that this is not a "vote" as such, but that it will be seriously considered in the final decision. If you are lucky, a preference will be clearly indicated. If not, the administration will be forced to make a decision with a divided staff, but at least staff will realize the factors involved and the complexity of the decision.

There are other possible approaches. For example, James E. Rush outlines several broad operational principles and then assigns weights to more specific requirements under each category. The three obvious categories are hardware, software and training. Rush lists the following items: operating system, characteristics, applications, database maintenance, functional integration, environmental integration and workstation training. He assigns a numeric value or weight to each. The total number of points for each system is then compared to a norm or average score.[5]

Checklist of Selection Criteria

However the library decides to rate the systems it is considering, it is helpful to have a checklist of selection criteria against which each IOLS can be measured.

After a review of more than 200 RFPs during a six-year period, Universal Library Systems (ULISYS) determined the following 23 basic requirements of an IOLS for academic and public libraries:[6]

1. The system should possess all of the capabilities of an online catalog, providing the power to search on any criteria, and should be easily expanded to include online public access replacing the card catalog.

2. The system should perform all the desired functions for circulation control online, with immediate updating of the files for fines, holds, renewal and overdue calculations.

3. Librarians on staff must be able to use their discretion and override the system when circumstances call for discretionary treatment of situations with the public.

4. The system must be very complete, including such areas as information and retrieval capability and other library services.

5. Flexibility with regard to the number of loan periods, media codes and patron types must be provided.

6. The system must be written in a standard, widely understood and used software language that can be readily programmed by library personnel, should the occasion rise.

7. Documentation of the software must be complete and available in the library itself at the time of software acceptance.

8. A standard industry-wide operating system readily understood by a wide number of people should be used.

9. The hardware provided should be of a type in common use and provided from within the United States.

10. The maintenance provided for hardware and software must be of the highest order and readily available from a local supplier of maintenance service.

11. It is essential that the system be available (up) more than 98% of the time.

12. A back-up procedure is required, which can ensure that the library is operational 100% of the time.

13. The system must be cost-effective to allow libraries to operate more efficiently given ever-increasing costs.

14. The quality of the training and operator's manuals provided must ensure the successful operation of the system by the library staff.

15. The system must be easy to use by librarians, staff and the public and, in addition, must be very flexible to allow for individual requirements.

16. Enhancements and improvements to the system should be continuously available to users.

17. A comprehensive system of backup and recovery is required so that if the database is destroyed, in the event of power disruption or for other reasons, it can be readily recreated.

18. All of the software necessary to complete the conversion and building of the database must be provided, along with the ability to interface with the various cataloging services (OCLC, WLN, UTLAS).

19. The vendor must be able to demonstrate reasonable financial stability, as well as a better than average chance to continue in business.

20. Communications interface capabilities should take advantage of the latest technology, to reduce communications costs.

21. Response time should be less than two seconds for 95% of all circulation transactions and less than five seconds for all inquiries. Response time should never exceed 10 seconds.

22. The hardware and operating system provided must allow for the capability to add such applications as payroll, accounts payable, general ledger and budget accounting, and word processing.

23. The proposing vendor should have at least two (preferably more) successfully operational installations.

It should be noted that even after bids have been received and the vendor selected, there is still room for negotiation. Once a vendor is sure that it has been selected, it may be more willing to negotiate costs. So although bids have been received and can be used as a basis for comparison, the bottom line has still not been reached. Substitution of terminals is one of the main areas where cost savings can be achieved without sacrificing functional ability or reliability. Lear Seigler and Hazeltine, along with other manufacturers, make a very serviceable, low cost terminal for around $600.

TRADE-OFFS

When selecting an IOLS, trade-offs are inevitable. There is not likely to be one system that meets all the library's current and anticipated needs. There are systems that will meet most of these needs, but they may lack some of the features you now have manually. For an IOLS, the *total* system and the way *all* subsystems interrelate must be considered. (In a single subsystem such as circulation or acquisitions, only the features of that subsystem need be considered.)

Comparing Subsystems

Instead of trading off one feature within a subsystem for another, one must decide which subsystem is primary, which is secondary, which is tertiary; then the relative features of each subsystem must be weighed against the total value of the system as a whole. For example, if circulation is the subsystem considered most important, then you may have to sacrifice some desirable public access catalog features to get an IOLS with the best circulation features.

The way in which the subsystems relate to each other is also important. Do all subsystems really use a common database? Does this database retain MARC format records, or does it need to? Or does the subsystem split the main bibliographic database into separate index files (discussed in Chapter 1) that are in a different format? These approaches have implications for both access time and the amount of disk storage space required. The more separate files in the system, the more storage space will be required. On the other hand, as noted in Chapter 2, accessing a file that contains only subject headings is obviously a lot faster than searching the whole shelflist record for subject headings each time the file is searched. As always, the integrated library system buyer is faced with trade-offs and compromises.

Hardware vs. Software

The trade-offs are further complicated by the varying speeds with which hardware operates, and the operating system on which the system runs, both of which affect efficiency. Current trends in hardware are toward physically smaller machines, with greater memory and faster operating speeds. Microcomputers have progressed from 8-bit to 16-bit to 32-bit capabilities. As previously stated, the higher the bits-per-word, the faster the operating system. At least in the microcomputer world, mass storage capacities are changing rapidly, almost monthly, from a few hundred thousand characters per disk to 10 megabyte and even 40 megabyte disks. All this is to say that hardware costs are generally coming down, either in terms of the price of the equipment itself or in terms of the increased capabilities available for the same price.

On the other hand, software costs are going up. VTLS marketed its software for $10,000 in 1980. As of 1984 it was charging $60,000. There is a reason for this increase. Software is labor-intensive and labor is costly, especially for programmers and systems analysts who presently command a premium wage. In order to be responsive to customer needs, new features and modules must be continually added. Authority control, Boolean search capability, etc., take time and personnel to develop and maintain. This is especially true for a noncommercial vendor such as a university, which frequently has to develop the program with existing staff who may also have other duties. There are certain built-in cost advantages for a commercial vendor, which has a full-time staff of programmers specifically to develop and maintain its software.

If a library is upgrading, the commercial vendor supplying the present system may have a distinct price advantage. If the library has already purchased or licensed the software, and is entitled to new releases, then that vendor can bid on the price of hardware alone. This fact is worth considering if the library wants to upgrade its system on a minimal budget. At the present time, this type of upgrade represents an immediate cost savings of $20,000 to $90,000 (the current price range for software packages)—enough to buy a considerable number of terminals.

MARC vs. Non-MARC Formats

The library may be faced with the possibility of trading a MARC-based system for a non-MARC-based one. If so, it must bear in mind that the ability to input and output MARC format records is essential for most academic and large libraries, and important if the system is likely to be replaced or upgraded. MARC format records are easier to transfer than non-standard or local format records.

There are many MARC formats (e.g., books, audiovisuals, maps, manuscripts, music, serials), not to mention variations such as UKMARC. (The latter could be important if the library is considering a system developed outside its own country based on UKMARC, for example.) Further, the Library of Congress has its own in-house version of MARC, and most networks or utilities have a slightly modified version, for example, OCLC/MARC.

To an academic librarian, storage of the record in non-MARC format is unthinkable, because every detail and piece of information is important. To most public libraries, the MARC format may be a useful vehicle for transporting a record to/from a network database, but not as important for local storage. To the special library in a corporate environment with a fixed-field orientation dealing with technical reports, which seeks to use local corporate computer equipment in a timeshare mode, MARC format is not as important. In fact, in some cases, it may not even be desirable.

This is not to diminish the importance of the MARC format as a communications vehicle and for creation of a union database. It is absolutely essential to have a standardized format for the transmission of bibliographic data. The existence of such a standard format, in fact, is one of the main contributing factors to the development of integrated online library systems. This same format also allows for differing local data records, since records can be reformatted as they are downloaded from a bibliographic utility. This, too, contributes to an integrated library system. If a library wants to use the full MARC record, it can do so. If it prefers an abbreviated record with more user-cordial labels than numeric tags, it can reformat the record. This flexibility makes the MARC format even more valuable.

SURVEY OF IOLS USERS

The survey reported here is intended to give readers an indication of the overall satisfaction with major IOLS systems and to identify the areas of least satisfaction. It is not intended to provide an evaluation of specific systems; rather, it gives a broad overview of libraries' experiences with integrated systems to date.

In May 1984, 70 users of integrated online library systems were surveyed to determine their degree of satisfaction with the systems. The survey population included 35 public libraries, 28 college and university libraries, 3 junior college libraries, 2 libraries for the blind and physically handicapped, and a state and national library. Fifty responses (71%) were received, with 45 of them, or 64%, usable. Unusable responses were from libraries in which the system was not yet operational. Systems reported on included: Biblio-Techniques Library and Information System, CL Systems Inc., Data Phases, Geac Ltd., IBM Dobis/Lueven, NOTIS, ULISYS and VTLS. The survey is reproduced in Figure 3.1 (on pages 49-50).

Among the respondents, 40 had circulation subsystems, 33 used cataloging subsystems, 20 had online public access catalogs, 15 had acquistions, 9 had serials subsystems and 9 had audiovisual materials booking. Virtually all subsystems were represented. Regarding system reliability, 60% of the respondents indicated that their system uptime was equal to or greater than 98%; 28% checked 95% to 97%; and 12% indicated uptime of less than 95%. Most had the system for a year or more. The causes of downtime were nearly equally divided between hardware and software, with hardware being slightly more frequent.

The majority of the respondents reported that service response time was within 24 hours. However, nine respondents reported software response time as greater than 48 hours, while only three reported the same response time for hardware. Eleven respondents reported software problems that were unresolved, but only two reported unresolved hardware problems. Hardware problems were usually resolved on the first call. Software problems required repeated visits or remained unsolved in more than 50% of the cases. The majority had service from the vendor, but three respondents used third party maintenance. Fourteen respondents (31%) had purchased software independent of hardware. Twelve respondents (26%) required on-site visits to resolve software problems. This could be significant if the vendor charges extra for on-site software visits.

Satisfaction with the system was rated on a scale of 1 to 10 with 10 being the highest or most satisfied. Satisfaction was measured in terms of the total system, in terms of hardware and software, separately and in terms of hardware and software maintenance. The average degree of satisfaction for all systems was 7.9 out of 10, with a range from 2 to 10. The software satisfaction average was 7.7, with a range of 3 to 10; hardware satisfaction averaged 8.4, with a range of 5 to 10.

Software maintenance was given the poorest rating of all categories at 6.9, with a range of 1 to 10. Hardware maintenance had a satisfaction indicator of 8.1, with a range of 3 to 10. A slim majority felt that their subsystems functioned exceptionally well together. Eighteen respondents or 40% felt that their subsystems functioned together with some difficulty. Only slightly less than half (49%) would recommend their systems without reservation; 44% with some reservation; 4% would not recommend their systems at all.

It appears that software development and maintenance are the areas of least satisfaction. Software is, of course, the most complex area of to debug and fix; problems are not readily resolved with a plug-in board, as is the case with hardware problems. Buyer's of systems should be aware of these problem areas, and current users should be consoled that many of their problems are not unique, but universal.

FOOTNOTES

1. James F. Corey, Helen L. Spalding and Jeanmarie Lang Fraser, "Involving Faculty and Students in the Selection of a Catalog Alternative," *Journal of Academic Librarianship* 8 (6) (January 1983): 328-333.

2. Ellen Miller, "Selecting Automated Library Systems in Academia: RFIs, RFPs, and Your Constituents," in *Conference on Integrated Online Library Systems, September 26-27, 1983: Proceedings,* rev. ed. (Canfield, OH: Genaway & Associates, Inc., 1984).

3. Joseph R. Matthews, "Competition and Change: the 1983 Automated Library System Marketplace," *Library Journal* 109 (8) (May 1, 1984): 853-860.

4. Karl Nyren and John Berry, "Information and Technology: At the Crossroads," *Library Journal* 108 (November 1, 1983): 20-21.

5. James E. Rush, "Evaluation of Integrated Online Library Systems," in *Conference on Integrated Online Library Systems, September 26-27, 1983: Proceedings,* rev. ed. (Canfield, OH: Genaway & Associates, Inc., 1984).

6. Reprinted courtesy of J.A. Speight, President, Universal Library Systems, #205, 1571 Bellevue Ave., West Vancouver, BC V7V 1A6.

Figure 3.1: IOLS User Survey

The population of this survey consists of librarians involved in the operation or management of an online library system.

The basic purpose of this survey is to obtain user evaluations of systems installed.

Data will be treated in aggregate for each system.

SYSTEM NAME: _____

SUBSYSTEMS USED (Check all applicable)
__ Acquisitions
__ AV materials booking
__ Catalog
__ Circulation
__ Online public access catalog
__ Serials
__ Other (specify)_____

TOTAL SYSTEM RELIABILITY (Check one)
_ Uptime 98% or more   _ Uptime 95 to 97%   _ Less than 95%
Time period used to measure uptime: _ 1 month _ 3 months _ 6 months
                                    _ 1 year   _ More than 1 year
    COMMENTS:_____

MOST FREQUENT CAUSES OF DOWNTIME (Check one)
_ Hardware   _ Software   Other (Specify)_____

SERVICE (Check one on each side)
    HARDWARE   **SOFTWARE**
    ___   Response within 24 hours   ___
    ___   Between 25 and 48 hours   ___
    ___   More than 48 hours   ___

    EQUIPMENT REPAIR PERSONNEL   **SOFTWARE SUPPORT PERSONNEL**

    ___   Knowledgeable   ___
    ___   Fixes problem on first call   ___
                  Requires repeated visits consultations
                      to fix problem

    ___   Problems remain unsolved   ___

COMMENTS:_____

SERVICE SUPPLIER(S) _ Turnkey vendor   _ Hardware manufacturer
                    _ Third party vendor   _ Software supplier

PROXIMITY OF FIELD REPRESENTATIVE FOR EQUIPMENT REPAIR
    _ Same city or less than 25 miles   _ 26 to 50 miles away
    _ 51 to 100 miles away   _ More than 100 miles away
    Do you use an acoustical coupler or a direct line to
        software support? _ YES   _ NO

Figure 3.1 (cont'd.)

User survey
Page 2

OTHER SUPPORT (Answer all applicable)

Do you have a systems support person (systems librarian or programmer with
    computer training or experience) on the library staff? _ YES _ NO
Do you use local computer staff outside of library staff? _ YES _ NO
Do software problems ever require on-site visits by
    software personnel? _ YES _ NO
Was software purchased independently from hardware? _ YES _ NO
Is software flexible, i.e. capable of modification and
    adaptation to local needs? _ YES _ NO

EVALUATION (Scale of 1 to 10. 10 highest or most satisfaction.)

Overall system satisfaction with total system? __
Overall satisfaction with software? __
Overall satisfaction with hardware? __
Overall satisfaction with software support services? __
Overall satisfaction with hardware maintenance service __

How well do the various subsystems function in relationship to each other?
    _ Exceptionally well _ With some difficulties __ Poorly or not at all

List features liked most by the staff:_____
_____

List features least liked:_____
_____

List desired features that are not available:_____
_____

Would you recommend this system for institutions similar to yours?
    _ Without reservation   _ With some reservation   _ Not recommended

PLEASE INDICATE DEGREE OF CONFIDENTIALITY:
    Responses may be identifed with our library? _ Yes _ No
    Responses should be treated confidentially without reference to our
      library? _ Yes _No

    RESPONDENT: _____
    TITLE:_____
    INSTITUTION:_____

4

System Implementation and Acceptance

The importance of implementation and acceptance was stated very clearly by Susan Baerg Epstein when she said: "This is frequently the most neglected area of integrated online library systems. Yet it is one of the most important. Implementation begins with conceptualization. If you don't allocate money for implementation, you will never optimize your system."[1] In other words, implementation begins, or at least should begin, when plans are first made to get an integrated online library system.

Frequently, no plans have been made for installing the computer system in a proper environment until after it has been obtained. According to Richard Stroum, vice president of customer service and support for CL Systems, Inc. (CLSI), these are hidden costs that are not brought up by either party until the contract has been signed. Sometimes this is done consciously, with the assumption that money that would not have been available if added on to the initial cost will somehow become available after the system is received. After all, the board cannot turn down the request for installation funds after it has approved the basic system. Sometimes installation costs have not been included in the original budget because they will be absorbed by other departments in the institution, such as the physical plant department at a university. More often than not, however, site preparation and other installation-related expenses were just not planned for.

According to Stroum, the key areas to consider when implementing an IOLS are reliability, flexibility and appearance. Environment is a prime factor in reliability. If the system is too hot or exceeds maintenance contract limits (usually 75 degrees is the maximum operating temperature), it is very likely to malfunction. If equipment does break down while operated under excessive temperatures, the vendor is not obligated to repair it under the maintenance contract. The library can have planned flexibility for the future, which will greatly reduce future costs, or be faced with unplanned expansion that will be much more costly. Finally, although seldom mentioned, appearance and neatness contribute to the efficient operation of a system.[2]

To these general considerations must be added contracts and vendor compliance, staff preparation and training, data conversion, scheduling and, finally, making the transition from one system to another. Each of these areas has a direct impact on the successful implementation of an IOLS. Let us examine them in more detail.

CONTRACTS

Much has been written about contractual agreements. Usually, the advice has run something to the effect that everything your library expects to be delivered must be in the contract. In addition, the document should contain provisions for acceptance testing and vendor compliance. These are all important issues, and there must be a legal contract which does spell out mutual obligations to protect both vendor and client. However, there are several additional points to consider.

Vendor-Client Relationship

The best contract in the world, containing the most detailed and specific clauses, does not prevent extended costly litigation in the event of failure of either party to comply. It has been said that the best contract is the one that can be put in a drawer and never looked at again. In other words, like a marriage contract, the validity and success of the relationship is as good as the two parties involved.

One way to ensure a smoother vendor-client relationship is to clearly define the responsibilities of each at the outset. One vendor, Universal Library Systems, Ltd., has drawn up a useful list of vendor-client responsibilities that can serve as a guide (see Figure 4.1).

Terms and Provisions

However good the working relationship may be, contracts are essential to provide legal assurance that the vendor will comply with its promises. (If vendors always resolved all problems in a satisfactory manner, contracts would not be necessary.) The payment terms will usually be specified in increments, with 10% to 25% of the total purchase price due upon installation and operation, and most of the balance due after an acceptance testing period (discussed in more detail, below). Some contracts require that the system operate consecutively for 60 to 90 days. Some restart the testing period if there is any failure during that time.

Be sure to determine if prices include transportation and installation, who is responsible for setting up the equipment and whether or not enhancements are part of maintenance agreements. Most contracts list the maintenance costs for the first year, and some indicate the rate of increase thereafter. Libraries are advised to check with other users of the system to determine actual increases.

Does the contract include preventive maintenance or only repair service? Is the vendor supplying the service directly or is it contracted to a third party? How far away is the nearest field repairman? Although it is generally suggested that the nearest technician be

Figure 4.1: Vendor-Client Responsibilities

Vendor's Responsibilities

1. To the best of its ability, to determine and recommend the correct hardware configuration for accommodating the bibliographic and patron files, the number of branches and the general scope of the system as described to it.

2. To modify its system where necessary to meet specific requirements of the individual library.

3. To collaborate with the library in systems testing and all phases of implementation.

4. To advise, where needed, on physical installation and site preparation.

5. To assist the library with ordering of bar-coded labels and other supplies.

6. To assist in the selection of communications facilities.

7. To advise on the most suitable conversion and data entry methods for books and borrowers.

8. To train library staff in operating the system.

9. To implement the system successfully.

Client Library's Responsibilities

1. To select a mutually agreeable project leader and not to change the leader without prior discussion with the vendor.

2. To order all supplies and materials, including bar-coded labels, library cards, disk packs, etc.

3. To provide an accurate and comprehensive database.

4. To organize and proceed with the building of the database.

5. To coordinate the placing of bar-coded or other labels on all books, library cards, etc.

6. To provide a sufficiently wide range of items and conditions to adequately test the system's programs and modifications.

7. To provide suitable physical accommodation for the equipment in time for the scheduled installation.

8. To order and install all necessary modems and data transmission lines.

9. To collaborate with the vendor in the systems testing, pilot running and implementation of the system.

Source: Courtesy of J.A. Speight, President, Universal Library Systems, #205, 1571 Bellevue Ave., West Vancouver, BC V7V 1A6.

located no more than 50 to 100 miles from the installation site, responsiveness is a more important factor than distance. A field representative who is 50 miles away and takes a week to respond is certainly not as good as a field representative who is 500 miles away but is on-site within 24 hours and orders replacement parts to arrive at the same time he does.

Training in the operations of the system is usually provided by a turnkey vendor. This includes software and hardware. If the system is sold independently, hardware training and software training or systems operation may be conducted separately by the computer manufacturer and the software vendor. Be sure you have checked the costs of each training session and whether or not they are included in the bid or quotation. Also, check to see if sessions are to be held at the vendor site (if turnkey), the software supplier's site or the hardware manufacturer's location. If off-site, the library will have to pay for staff travel time. If on-site, the library may have to pay travel expenses for the software or hardware vendor. In some cases, travel is included.

Problems

Problems can occur when the desired vendor will not agree to some aspect of the contract, such as the testing period. What do you do? Do you drop that vendor and go to another one, tie up the arrival of the system for days or weeks in precontract negotiation or "litigation," or reconcile yourself to the fact that users of that system rate the system high and have never had a problem? One software vendor has a clause that states that obligations can be dropped by either party at any time "without cause." A hardware vendor states that acceptance testing of its equipment shall be performed by its own engineers, on-site. Mutual trust must be the starting point. If you are bogged down in negotiation and litigation before the relationship begins, trust is lacking.

The reader should not mistake the above as saying that contracts are not essential, but rather that the overall integrity of the vendor is as important as the contract itself. It would be wise to check corporate records for excessive previous and outstanding litigation. If there is a continuous history of litigation in the corporate background, one might be more cautious. (On the other hand, corporations change and litigation may be left over from previous management. Also, the larger a corporation becomes, the more vulnerable it is to lawsuits. Therefore, always investigate the circumstances.)

Bear in mind that, sometimes, vendors over-promise and clients over-wish. Even administrators may make promises to funding agencies that can't be kept. Libraries must be careful to investigate whether their demands can realistically be met. They must also take steps to ensure vendor compliance with the contract. Selecting a good project manager is one way to accomplish this. The project manager should be a person of some authority who is willing to learn, put in long hours and be empowered to cross divisional lines. Compensation should match this increased responsibility.

ENVIRONMENT FOR THE IOLS

The library must pay close attention to the physical requirements of an IOLS. These include site preparation, space requirements, fire and safety factors, and security.

Space Requirements

To begin with, it is important to allow enough space to house the IOLS even if you already have a computer installation. Your present room may be adequate for a single subsystem computer, but insufficient when it is converted to a total integrated system. An IOLS usually requires additional peripherals. For example, if a library with abbreviated circulation records in short, fixed-field format converts to full MARC record storage for an online public catalog, much more disk space will be needed. More disks require more disk drives, which in turn require additional space (and air conditioning).

Typically, about four feet of space should be allowed in and around the computer system. Remember, disk drives are like file cabinet drawers; they pull out. Enough room must also be allowed for a service representative to work in front of and around the disk drive when it is extended. Storage space should also be taken into account, for such items as supplies (overdue notices, etc.) and backup disks. (It should be noted here that the library should always keep a "bank copy" of backup disks, updated weekly, at another location *outside* the library.)

Site Preparation

Construction, wiring, temperature control and fire protection are all part of site preparation for an IOLS.

Construction

Librarians should work with the building contractors and insist that specifications are met. One person should be named as a liaison between the vendor, the library and the contractor. Contractors sometimes have a tendency to ignore specifications. Access to phone lines, power sources and ventilation ducts are some of the fixed constraints that will be encountered.

The complexity of cabling increases the size of the system. A raised floor will allow the cabling to fit underneath the work area and prevent anyone from tripping on or damaging it. A raised floor also eliminates the need to relocate electrical outlets when changes or additions are made.

If raised floors are not used, plastic floor tiles should be used because they dissipate voltage and static electricity, which can damage disks and destroy components. Every attempt should be made to avoid carpeting the computer area. However, if carpets must be used, then anti-static carpets should surround the terminals and the computer system. Other less obvious considerations are the load factor of the equipment and the floor, the size of equipment and the size of the elevator, if needed. Can the system be brought into the building?

Acoustic tile ceilings are good for sound dampening, but if any repairs have to be made in wiring, or there are any water pipes above the tiles, problems could arise. The particles of dust that fall when acoustic tiles are removed have been known to cause a system crash. All equipment should be turned off and covered before any repairs are made to the ceiling in the computer room.

Next to electrical difficulties, *dust* is the second major enemy of disk drives. Dust clogs filters and reduces air flow. If a positive pressure is kept in the computer room it will act as a seal to keep dust out.

Wiring

Dedicated circuitry with wiring going directly to the main power source for the building and a circuit breaker panel is essential. The system should be grounded separately, directly onto the frame of the building. Scheduling of computer activities should be planned so as not to conflict with peak periods of electrical use in the community. In one library, problems occurred regularly in the afternoon at the time when generators "kicked in." There should be a single power switch, and lines should be conditioned so that power is clean—i.e., protected from surges or spikes, brownouts and blackouts. Line conditioning may cost $3000 to $4000, but can save added expense in the long run. The computer should be located in an area free from electrical noise. For example, don't put it next to a copying machine or next door to a transformer. Even radio station transmitting antennas have been known to affect the performance of computer systems.

The library is responsible for the installation of data cable. Extra cable in the ceilings or enroute to the terminals will allow for the addition of more terminals at a later date with minimum difficulty. Do not run these cables in the same conduit with power lines. The terminals should be located where there is minimum glare; avoid direct sunlight. Cathode ray terminals (CRTs) can interfere with the operation of theft detection systems and should not be located closer than 15 feet if at all possible.

Temperature Control

Adequate air conditioning and temperature control are very important. A common sense guide for environmental conditions is to relate them to what people would need. If conditions are too extreme for humans they are probably not good for computers either. Stroum recommends that temperatures range between 65 and 75 degrees, humidity from 40% to 80% non-condensing, and there should be 7.5 to 8 atmospheric changes per hour.[3] Without air changes, heat envelopes are likely to develop, creating unequal heating or cooling of the equipment. Remember that British Thermal Units (BTUs), the unit of measure to determine the heat generated by an object, are a factor not only of the equipment itself, but also of the number of people in the room, the size of the room and the amount of insulation in the walls. (Be aware that additional air conditioning may contribute to a slight increase in insurance costs.)

Fire Protection

Dry Halon, which is nonconductive and noncorrosive, is the best type of fire extinguisher to use. Halon extinguishers cost from $1000 to $3000 to refill. The fire alarm and sprinkler systems should be triggered by temperature, not smoke. If a system is attended, smoke should set off an alarm to alert operators, but not trigger the fire extinguishing system. Unattended systems should have an automatic dial to the fire department or security office, which will operate if the system is not reset in 20 seconds.

PERSONNEL AND POLICY CHANGES

Other important aspects of implementation are planning for policy changes and training and orienting personnel. Susan Epstein has stated that policy and personnel planning should begin when the system is first considered, since a new system will force changes in policy and personnel.

Staff Orientation and Training

As Epstein states, "If the policies manual does not need revision then you have not taken full advantage of the system." You have not gained a great deal if you have merely mechanized a manual system and have not improved it. Staff need to be trained, need to realize that there will be downtime and need to be able to deal with angry patrons when errors occur.[4]

There is a myth about automation, built up by early proponents, that should be dispelled. Society has long been told that "computers do not make mistakes, only people do." If staff members begin working with an integrated system believing that there will never be any mistakes, errors or downtime, it will be a lot more difficult for them to accept these occurrences when they happen. Staff must accept the concept of downtime. If the library is switching from one automated system to another, or upgrading an existing system, acceptance will be a lot easier because of previous experience. If, however, the library is automating for the first time it will be doubly important that staff understand this concept.

In a manual system, several different files were created by each department. An IOLS will eliminate these separate files and require more standardization and training. Management should be frank with the staff in terms of the changes that the IOLS will bring about. In most cases, the clerical staff will not lose their jobs but the nature of their work will change. The transition period will require even more work. Creating a separate test file for staff to "play" with will help them become familiar with the system without affecting the database. People learn at different rates and allowances should be made for this. Build on previous training and let staff members know that they are only expected to learn 10% at a time. Force staff to look at and examine operations. What do they do and why? Examine policies in relationship to automated procedures.

Policies and Procedures

This is the time to establish new rules for the computer room, if the old ones have been violated, never established or not enforced. No smoking or drinking should be allowed: smoke can gradually "gum up" parts and spilled drinks can cause even greater catastrophies. Security, a part of any computer operation, takes on added importance with an IOLS. Remember, the whole MARC record bibliographic file is now vulnerable instead of just a portion of the file. Access to the computer room should be tightly controlled. If the IOLS is housed in a separate room, the door should be kept closed. In reality, good security depends as much on the personnel that will be working with the computer system as it does on bolts and locks.

DATA CONVERSION

"All systems should be looked at through data conversion eyes," according to Gail Persky of Bobst Library, New York University.[5] Will the new system require data lacking in your records? Can the new system use the same bar codes or other item codes that are presently used? Some systems cannot handle serials, multi-volume sets, variant editions or copies. (One library lost all of its information on multi-volume sets because of this.)

Prior to conversion, consider future as well as present uses of data. In addition, a decision should be made as to whether data "cleanup" will take place during or after conversion. "Do not recreate a manual system in machine-readable form."[6]

Creating the Database

The most important—and the most time-consuming—aspect of converting records is building the bibliographic database. The next most important step is to attach item codes to each copy of each title. Third (though some may consider this second), the database must be "cleaned," whereby authority files are constructed and the entire database is verified for accuracy, completeness and currentness of information.

Data conversion may be substantially easier if you are upgrading from, say, a circulation system to an integrated system with the same vendor instead of switching vendors. Loading MARC tapes may not vary in difficulty from one vendor to another, but attaching existing bar code labels from one vendor's database to another vendor's database may be much more complex. The source of the bibliographic record must be identified (OCLC, RLIN, etc.) to determine the format and tape configuration.

In addition to titles, two other types of records are needed: authority records and patron records. Public libraries might use the voter registration list; corporate libraries can convert from the employee file; and academic libraries can use the student, faculty and staff files.

If the library plans to use archive tapes, and they have been stored for several years, find out the condition of the tapes *before* duplicating them. If the format has changed over the years, get copies of all changes in the tape specifications and headers. Specifications for conversion should cover all elements of both the old data format and the new. Use a chart to move field by field if necessary. Testing of earlier and later tapes should also be conducted. Hand-select known problem records and try to process them. Correct records and then retest.

Determine the degree of staff involvement and whether to convert in-house or to farm-out conversion to a vendor. There are several agencies that will assist in conversions of data. First, a bibliographic utility (OCLC, RLIN, WLN, etc.) may be able to provide your library with MARC tapes if the library has been inputting records into the utility's database. Second, the library's local network may be able to generate such tapes if the utility cannot.

Commercial services provide a third option for converting the library's records. Autographics, Inc. (which was recently designated as a utility) provides retrospective conversion service with local online database management through AGILE II. Data from library's Autographics, OCLC, RLIN, etc., archival tapes are available online for local access to bibliographic records and holdings. It interfaces with all major circulation systems, and authority control is available.[7]

Carrollton Press, Inc., through its REMARC database, provides local conversion by creating a local retrospective archival tape while matching a library's search parameters against LC-MARC and REMARC. Archival tapes are sent to the library on a regular basis. LC-MARC/REMARC is also available through Dialog Information Services, Inc.[8] Inforonics Library Information Automation Service (ILIAS) provides access to its LC-MARC tapes online. It will produce catalog cards via a profile or archival tapes, and circulation tapes from any archival tape. It also provides repetitive searching of search codes/requests against new LC-MARC tapes for a time period or until a match is made.[9]

Whatever type of service is chosen, compare the database used by the vendor for similarities to your library's holdings, and determine whether the search strategies and services meet your requirements.

Testing the Database

Usually, a test or pilot database will be developed before running conversion on all records. It is extremely important to test processes and the accuracy of records frequently, starting with a small number of records at first. It is easier to identify and correct a small file than a big one. Also, other problems may emerge as more records are added to the database, and it is easier to correct one problem at a time than to solve a host of errors or aberrations all at once. This pilot project should be conducted before the system is delivered.

It is important to schedule the conversion project and to frequently compare the rate of progress with the schedule. Ruth C. Carter and Scott Bruntjen, in *Data Conversion,* outline the planning and scheduling process for a data conversion project. Comparative methods as well as common pitfalls are discussed.[10] The smoothness of the implementation of data conversion will be directly related to the preparation made for it. Finally, satisfaction with the IOLS, and the amount of problems encountered, will be directly related to the thoroughness of database testing.

ACCEPTANCE TESTING

Formal acceptance is the library's agreement that the vendor has fulfilled the contract, according to Cathryn Nook and Nancy Norton.[11] They feel a well-defined acceptance test period should precede acceptance, and an acceptance test should be a part of the contract. Acceptance testing should include as many days as possible of consecutive uptime (20 or 30 days are usually suggested) with the stipulation that the whole period starts over in the event the system fails at any time.

Although the last step in the procurement process, the acceptance test should be the first in the contract and even be included in the RFP. The content of the acceptance test should include: reliability, a full test of the operating system, telecommunications testing, loading the database, all component subsystems and response time.

Diagnostics should be run on each piece of equipment before it leaves the vendor's site. Responsibility for downtime should be spelled out. Downtime normally starts when the vendor is notified; scheduled maintenance is not considered downtime. Keep a detailed log of all downtime and the reasons for it. As part of the test, bring the system completely down, recover and verify restoration of service without loss of data and backup devices. This tests how the system will respond in an emergency situation, not just under normal operating conditions.

If you have telephone ports, test them. Verify the loading of records, and check for the appropriate number of copies and the correctness of the call number. Specify the percent of the database that must be loaded before testing begins. Load as large and as representative a database as possible. Test updating, online and batch processing, and each subsystem, including branch operations. Test all functions, even ones that you do not intend to use immediately. There should also be some provisions for testing enhancements as they become available.

Response time is measured from the time a command is sent until the first character appears on the screen, or until the entire response is displayed. Test the system's response time while background operations are being performed as well.

Schedule the testing period from the time when the vendor says the system is installed and operational. The testing period typically ends 30 to 60 days later. Throughout the acceptance testing period, both the vendor and the library should issue written progress reports. Also, *do not go online until staff are trained in basic functions and operation.* Prior to the start of the test, staff should be thoroughly trained, technical manuals and documentation should be delivered and reviewed, and the collection should be bar-coded. The amount of time devoted to test preparation will be reflected in the success of the tests and satisfaction with the system.[12]

SCHEDULING

A schedule should be established at the time of the contract. Typically, it will include the following steps:

- Project planning;
- User and management training;
- Specifications and library requirements;
- Site inspection and preparation;
- Ordering of computer equipment, supplies and cabling;
- Receipt and testing of equipment;
- Hardware and software testing;
- Bringing up the system;
- Loading patron data;
- Loading bibliographic data;
- Adding or changing all item labels;
- Entering item data;
- Installing communications gear;
- Installing and operating branch systems;
- Turning over documentation to buyer;
- Turning over the system;
- Wrapup meetings with the project leader and staff; and
- A final check with the library management.

Figure 4.2 presents a typical implementation schedule for an IOLS.

TRANSITION TO AN IOLS

Making a smooth transition from the present system to the IOLS translates, in most cases, as making the switch with the least amount of downtime possible. The library can do several things to make this process go more smoothly. First, identify interdependent items and arrange for them early on. For example, it may take 90 days lead time to get telecommunications links installed, and the same amount of time to get item or patron labels from the supplier. Second, identify bottlenecks and have backup plans ready; this is especially important for integrated systems. A primary rule to follow is: *Do not install all the subsystems at once.* As noted earlier, the primary module that motivates selection of the system is the one that will drive the system and should be implemented first. Make sure one subsystem is up and running well before implementing the next one.[13]

In some cases, problems are unavoidable. For example, it may not be possible to run two systems simultaneously—there may only be adequate room in the computer room for one system at a time, and the electrical demands and air conditioning requirements may be too great to be supported by the current environment. In this case, the transition may be less smooth. Then, too, if a library is switching vendors, not all are willing to assist in the transition or make a graceful exit when another vendor has been chosen. If a library finds itself in this situation, it should see to it that the transition is swift and well-thought-out, with data converted off-site prior to the arrival of the new system.

Figure 4.2: Sample Implementation Schedule

Time in Weeks From Date of Issuance of Notice to Proceed ⟶

	1	2	3	4	5	6	7	8	9	10	11	12	13	14	15	16	17	18	19	20	21	22	23	24	25	26	27	28
Starting Date		x																										
Conversion Discussion			x																									
Required Facility Readiness				x																								
Equipment Delivery					x																							
Equipment Installation						x																						
Software Installation						x																						
Data Base Expansion Bibliographic							x---	---	---	---	---x																
Data Base Transfer – Patron Information						x																						
Implement Online Catalog Parameter Training – Acquisitions & Online Catalog											x		x															
Installation Training – Acquisitions & Online Catalog							x						x															
Online Training													x															
Acceptance-Function							x---	---	---	---	---	---x																
Acceptance-Reliability														x														
System fully operational (Circulation, Acquisitions and Public Access Catalog)														x														

Source: CL Systems, Inc. Reproduced with permission.

FOOTNOTES

1. Susan Baerg Epstein, "Impact of Implementing New IOLS on Staff, Policies, and Procedures," in *Conference on Integrated Online Library Systems, September 26-27, 1983: Proceedings,* rev. ed. (Canfield, OH: Genaway & Associates, Inc., 1984).

2. Richard P. Stroum, "Installation, Site Preparation, and Environmental Control," in *Conference on Integrated Online Library Systems, September 26-27, 1983: Proceedings,* rev. ed. (Canfield, OH: Genaway & Associates, Inc., 1984).

3. Stroum, op. cit.

4. Epstein, op. cit.

5. Gail Persky, "Data Conversion for an Integrated Library System," in *Conference on Integrated Online Library Systems, September 26-27, 1983: Proceedings,* rev. ed. (Canfield, OH: Genaway & Associates, Inc., 1984).

6. Persky, op. cit.

7. Ibid.

8. Ibid.

9. Ruth C. Carter and Scott Bruntjen, *Data Conversion* (White Plains, NY: Knowledge Industry Publications, Inc., 1983).

10. Ibid.

11. Cathryn R. Nook and Nancy Norton, "Acceptance Test for an Integrated Library System," in *Conference on Integrated Online Library Systems, September 26-27, 1983: Proceedings,* rev. ed. (Canfield, OH: Genaway & Associates, Inc., 1984).

12. Nook and Norton, op. cit.

13. Epstein, op. cit.

5

The IOLS Vendor Survey

Acquiring an integrated online library system is a complex decision which the library will have to live with for several years to come. Even with the most careful research and the involvement of many staff members, it is still possible to find that essential features that were "being developed, forthcoming or scheduled to be operational" are missing when the IOLS is installed.

There are no better words to use when considering any computer system than "show me" and "is it operational and available now?" The number of offerings in the integrated library system marketplace is changing almost monthly, as new systems or enhancements are developed. As Richard De Gennaro noted: "We will never have a finished total integrated library system, because we will never be satisfied to freeze the systems when we know that further improvements will always be possible."[1]

SURVEY METHODOLOGY

In an effort to obtain more information about the current status of the various systems, the author undertook a survey of selected vendors of 32 systems. The survey was first conducted in spring 1983 and was updated in April 1984.

The most authoritative source was sought at each vendor to complete the survey. In addition, the author attempted to verify the information given through personal conversations and a check of the literature on IOLS. In order to keep the survey concise and easy to respond to, a format was used which allowed most questions to be answered by checking the appropriate column. The survey is reproduced in Figure 5.1 at the end of this chapter.

Incidentally, a library could use this survey form as an abbreviated request for information or in lieu of an RFP. It is easy to fill out and allows a large amount of significant data to be compiled in tabular format. All the vendor has to do is place check marks in the appropriate spots. Keep in mind, however, that the respondent is typically a marketing person: Although not likely to be dishonest, he or she may be inclined to be overly optimistic about available versus planned operations, as well as development times. Care should be taken to verify information supplied by the vendor to make sure that definitions are the same for both the respondent and the surveyor. A simple phone call to users will also help substantiate current availability of items. (Most vendor proposals or quotations contain or should contain a list of system users.)

A brief summary of the results of this survey of vendor systems will be presented in this chapter. (Specific vendors will be discussed in Chapter 6.) A composite summary of the results of the survey is given in Appendix A. Information on some systems was too new to allow time for a survey; in such cases, information is based on vendor literature and/or personal contact by the author. A complete list of *all* vendors included in this book can be found in Appendix B. The reader is urged to consult vendors directly for the most up-to-date information.

SURVEY TERMINOLOGY AND FORMAT

For the purpose of the survey, the term "integrated online library system" was defined as "any library system that uses a common machine-readable database and has two or more subsystems operational and accessible online, such as circulation, public catalog, acquisitions, etc."

The survey sought to determine the actual operational status of systems and subsystems and, hence, the current state of the art of integrated online library systems. All subsystems or modules and operations had four status categories that could be checked:

• "Operational and available" means the subsystem, function or operation is running and can be purchased and installed at this moment. It is designated by OA.

• "Operational but not available" means this function is operating as a pilot project somewhere but is not available until testing is complete. It is designated by ONA.

• "Under development" means that these operations are in the process of being developed, but are not operational even as a pilot project or at a test site. This category is designated by UD.

A fifth column was provided for the estimated date of availability (EDA) if a system was in the planning stage or under development. Readers should note that the "operational but not yet available" category often refers to systems that have been operating in the pilot testing stage, but in which "bugs" are discovered, which sends the system back to the drawing board. Therefore, systems or subsystems that are designated as operational but not available, or as under development, should be evaluated with some caution.

Part One of the survey was concerned with the overall status of the various subsystems, such as acquisitions, cataloging, etc., (e.g., Can you buy it now? When will it be available?). Part Two sought functional information about the IOLS in general (e.g., Can it process MARC records? Does it retain MARC records?). Part Three obtained information on the specific functions and operations within each subsystem (e.g., Does the acquisitions package have fund accounting? Does the catalog subsystem have an authority file?). Although not a subsystem as such, the ability of the IOLS to generate management data was also queried in Part Three (e.g., Can statistics on "throughput" or the number of items passing through the system or subsystem be obtained by subsystem? Will the IOLS record the number of system overrides which could mean that policies, procedures or security measures may need to be reconsidered?).

The last section of the survey obtained brief data on the nature of the system (turn-key, software only, etc.), brand of hardware and whether or not the equipment is modified. It also asked for basic information about the location of training programs (on or off-site) and the number of installations.

FINDINGS

It was sometimes difficult to neatly categorize all responses. In some cases, vendors checked more than one status category, usually with a valid explanation. For example, Data Phase has an operational online public access catalog, but is developing it in two phases. The first phase provides author/title access and is available. The second phase provides subject and call number access, but is operational and not yet available. Since the basic online public access catalog is available, OA has been indicated in the summary of results given in Appendix A. (Another example is NOTIS, which has a circulation subsystem operational and available, but is in the process of developing a newer version.) Finally, it should be noted that not every vendor answered every category.

As expected, the three subsystems that are listed as operational by nearly all vendors are circulation, cataloging and an online public access catalog. Acquisitions is the next most frequently offered subsystem. Fund accounting, as allied to acquisitions, ranks next. The number of vendors offering serials subsystems is limited. Although most vendors indicated that a serials subsystem is planned, most gave projected dates of arrival which were months or a year into the future. At the time of the survey, no vendor had all subsystems (including serials) fully operational and available.

The majority of systems can transfer a full MARC record into the local database directly. Most retain the full MARC record, however some do reformat it. Only about 50% of the systems generate management statistics. Some allow users to compile their own reports through general statistical packages available on their computers as part of the general operating system package of software.

All systems have some form of back up; most use tape or disk backup. Some also produce a COM catalog. A number of vendors offer uninterrupted power supply (UPS) systems or power failure recovery systems.

The findings for specific subsystems are reviewed briefly below.

Circulation

Since circulation subsystems are one of the most well-developed, this category contained the longest list of items. Nearly all of the circulation subsystems available can provide online check-in/check-out to maintain inventory control, maintain a record of activity, place holds, compute fines and credit payments. Circulation functions for branches can be maintained, and there is a provision for varying loan periods. Nearly all systems can accept bar code input, some can accept OCR-A type font. The NOTIS system still accommodates punched cards and magnetic strips.

Several systems are unable to generate circulation statistics by patron category and format category. Nearly all provide online displays of patron or book status, can indicate item status on the display in the public catalog mode and can print lists of missing items or overdues. Nearly all systems can display items charged to patrons, requests by patrons and the item status in the online catalog. (The Avatar system also indicates which return book truck the item is on.) The maximum number of patron records, books or other materials that can be accommodated is related to the capacity of the hardware. Almost all systems can provide access to item records by call number, author, item code and title, and can also provide access to patron records by patron identification number.

Cataloging

Several items were considered in cataloging. Can any file in the record be modified? Is there full screen editing? What are the different access points to the record, author and title, OCLC, RLIN, added entries, etc.? Is there a workform for original cataloging? Can an authority file be created while loading MARC records? Does the authority file, if available, have the capability of global changes or deletions? Can the record indicate various locations such as branch libraries? Does the system allow for direct input of the item record from a bar code reader?

Most of the above capabilities are available on the majority of integrated library systems. Access by RLIN or OCLC number and ISBN number are under development at Northwestern. The authority file is operational but not available in the Geac and Data Research Associates (DRA) systems, and under development by CLSI and Data Phase. A workform is operational and available in most systems. Bar code reader capability for cataloging is under development at Northwestern and planned by M/A COM.

Online Public Access Catalog

Although most of the functions of an online catalog are similar, there are slight variations in features and definitions. One vendor said that it did not have an online catalog. Further questioning revealed that the "inquiry" mode of its circulation system is functioning virtually as an online catalog. Readers should bear in mind that, as with many of the terms used throughout the survey form, there may be slightly different interpretations of terms on the part of the respondent and the surveyor (although for the most part they are fairly accepted terms in the library world).

Basically, the survey sought to determine whether the online public access catalog subsystem could search records by author, title, uniform title, added entries, subject headings, series or any MARC tag. Nearly all respondents indicated that their systems can provide access by all of these fields. When it comes to Boolean searches using operators such as AND, OR, NOT or combined terms, fewer systems have this capability.

DRA has an "implicit" Boolean search capability, and Boolean searches are now available on VTLS. Both the NOTIS and VTLS systems can search via truncated terms, and VTLS can conduct an "instring" Boolean search. Avatar and M/A COM claim that "instring searching" will find the term regardless of location in the string or field searched. These same systems provide "full text searching" to find the term regardless of where it is located in the record.

Nearly all systems have the capability of "browsing" by author, subject or title. All but NOTIS and Carlyle permit browsing in the shelf list or by call number. The way in which browsing is conducted, or the specific procedures involved, vary considerably. Some systems display each item on a single line, some list the total number of items and then display four or five of these at a time on the screen.

The status of an item (on order, in process, available for circulation, checked out or on a cart, branch location, etc.) can be displayed by the majority of systems. Most systems surveyed allow access by phone using an acoustical coupler. Nearly all can display upper/lower case, abbreviated records, full and partial records. Most can handle ALA character set and can display records on a terminal with that set.

Acquisitions

Fifteen integrated systems have an acquisitions subsystem operational and available. A number of functions were queried in the survey. Can the order status of items be indicated in the public access catalog, so the inquirer can determine whether or not the item sought has been ordered, received or is in cataloging? Does the system provide an interactive workform for original items not in the network? Can the system generate claims for orders and maintain an in-process file by date, vendor or title? Are there provisions for handling special orders, such as approval plans, standing orders, memberships and exchange agreements?

Serials

Ten vendors indicated that a serials subsystem of some sort is available or operational. Of those, only NOTIS has check-in and claiming ability. Current acquisitions are shown by NOTIS in the public catalog and Data Research Associates can show the ordering and claiming of titles, and can create a union list in print form (COM) or online.

Fund Accounting

Fund accounting features are limited to those systems with an acquisition subsystem. Information was obtained on a number of items. Can the system maintain and modify records for multiple accounts, give a balance sheet or ledger display, and account for encumbrances, expenditures and free balances. In addition, can funds be credited and debited, encumbered or disencumbered? Can the system handle prepayments? How are accounting records accessed? By account number, vendor, fund name, date, invoice number, name and title? Are financial summary reports generated? What about audit trails to assist in monitoring funds?

Administrative or Management Information

The function of providing administrative information is sometimes known as a decision support system. The inability to capture throughput data on activities of the system (e.g., number and type of terminals used, number of books ordered, etc.) is a general weakness of automated library systems and libraries in general. Historically, libraries have not retained much data beyond the number of books cataloged or in the collection (possibly by LC number or subject category), and the total number of items circulated. Hence, many libraries know little about the activities of their staff and patrons. (The number of libraries that do not even compile a library-wide annual report is surprising.)

The systems offered by Data Phase, M/A COM, Geac and Data Research Associates allow for some kinds of management information, such as order price versus actual price in acquisitions, time to fill information and number of orders generated. Summary data on patrons, item codes and activity by subject category and/or branch are available on most. C L Systems has a very detailed breakdown of activity by each type of patron and assigned subject categories according to classification.

These statistics can be extremely valuable to library administrators. From a management point of view, statistics are most helpful in measuring use and determining future needs and directions. For example, a library can determine whether the use of the collection in a particular subject area has continued to increase on a per capita basis. The number of system overrides, if reported, might also provide a clue as to whether overdues and fines are being reduced without full authorization, or whether the system needs adjustment.

Only six of the systems surveyed provide statistics on type of terminal activity: How frequently is a specific terminal used? What is the nature of its use—author, title, subject search, help screens, etc.? Good statistics regarding use also provide strong documentation for obtaining funds or additional funds for the library.

Information on the nature of the IOLS (turnkey, software-only, etc.), the type of equipment it operates on and the number and type of installations could not be summarized in Appendix A. However, this information is given for each system in the detailed vendor profiles appearing in Chapter 6.

FOOTNOTES

1. Richard DeGennaro, "Library Automation and Networking: Perspectives on Three Decades," *Library Journal* 108(7) (April 1, 1983): 631.

Figure 5.1: Survey of Integrated Online Library Systems

PURPOSE: To determine the current state of the art of integrated online library systems.

INTEGRATED ONLINE LIBRARY SYSTEM refers to any library system that uses a common machine readable database and has two or more subsystems operational and accessible online, such as circulation, public catalog, acquisitions, etc.

METHOD: This survey is being sent to each vendor known to market a system meeting the above requirements.

DEFINITIONS

ACCOUNT: Used for budget line such as 950 Books, 951 Periodicals, 952 Microforms, etc. and vendor accounts such as Baker & Taylor, Wiley, etc.

FUND: Areas with a budget allocation. Departments, schools, colleges, branches, etc. are examples of areas with budget allocations.

ONLINE PUBLIC CATALOG: Online public access catalog. Any form of public catalog that allows access to the library's bibliographic records by multiple access points via a computer terminal.

INSTRUCTIONS
   Please place a check mark under the appropriate status for each subsystem or operation where a line extends across the page under status categories. The term status is used to describe the current capability of the system. The four levels of status are abbreviated as defined below and are headers at the top of each page.
   If there is no line across the page and a question mark follows, answer the question directly. If a yes or no or multiple answer is required, circle applicable response. If a direct answer is called for put answer right after question.

STATUS INDICATORS

   OA (OPERATIONAL AND AVAILABLE): This subsystem, function, or operation
      is running and can be purchased and installed at this moment.

   ONA (OPERATIONAL BUT NOT AVAILABLE): Operating as a pilot project
      somewhere but not available until testing is complete.

   UD (UNDER DEVELOPMENT): In the process of being developed but is not
      operational even as a pilot project or at a test site.

   PLANNED: PLANNED FOR DEVELOPMENT at some future date.

   EDA: ESTIMATED DATE OF AVAILABILITY, if planned.

Figure 5.1 (cont'd.)

	OA	ONA	UD	PLANNED	EDA
PART ONE. SUBSYSTEMS					
ACQUISITIONS					
AV MATERIALS BOOKING					
CATALOGING					
CIRCULATION					
FUND ACCOUNTING					
ONLINE PUBLIC ACCESS CATALOG					
SERIALS CONTROL					
PART TWO. SYSTEM (GENERAL)					
Online interface with bibliographic utility (OCLC, RLIN, etc.)					
Ability to transfer MARC record from utility directly into in-house database.					
Full MARC? YES NO CIRCLE ONE.					
Partial MARC only? YES NO					
Is FULL MARC record retained in in-house database? YES NO					
Is record reformatted? YES NO					
Can MARC records be loaded from tapes? YES NO					
Various levels of access:					
View record					
Edit (modify) record					
Delete record					
Generate management reports:					
Accounting					
Throughput statistics					
Items processed					
Terminal use					
By search type					
Subject					
Author					
Title					
Backups: COM Disk Tape Printouts					
Other (specify)					
Other system wide features (Specify):					

Figure 5.1 (cont'd.)

	OA	ONA	UD	PLANNED	EDA
PART THREE. SPECIFIC FUNCTIONS, OPERATIONS					
ACQUISITIONS					
Online interactive with OPAC, i.e. able to change item status on OPAC record to indicate:					
On-order					
Received					
Bindery					
Other (specify)					
Display online interactive work form with prompts for original items					
Generate (print) orders					
Provision for claiming orders based on EDA					
Provison for processing:					
Approval plans					
Standing orders					
Memberships					
Exchange agreements					
Maintain in-process file by:					
Date					
Vendor					
Title					
Provision for donor file with addresses, amounts, etc.					
Other (specify and indicate status)					
FUND ACCOUNTING					
Ability to maintain and modify records for several accounts					
Maximum number of accounts/funds allowable?					
Balance or ledger sheet display of accounts					
Balance or ledger sheet display of funds					
Ability to maintain and display funds and accounts by budgeted amount					
For each account display:					
Encumbrances (outstanding orders)					
Expenditures (actual payments)					
Free or unencumberd balance					
Abilty to:					
Credit/debit accounts/funds					
Encumber/disencumber account/funds					

Figure 5.1 (cont'd.)

	OA	ONA	UD	PLANNED	EDA
FUND ACCOUNTING (CONTINUED)					
Capability of handling prepayments					
Provision for access to fund or accounting records by:					
Account number or category (950,951,etc.)					
Vendor name and/or account number					
Fund name (Biology department, branch, friends, etc.)					
Date of issue					
Invoice number					
Author/Title					
Audit trails					
Can generate financial summary reports:					
Total fund actitivy					
Total account activity					
Other (specify and indicate status)					
CATALOGING					
Ability to modify any field in record					
Full screen editing					
Access to records by:					
Author					
Title					
OCLC/RLIN no.					
ISBN					
ISSN					
Added entries					
Subject headings					
Authority file					
Global find					
Global delete/add					
Authority file creation while loading MARC records					
Workform display with prompts for original cataloging					
Ability to indicate various locations:					
Branch libraries					
Multiple campuses					
Allow for direct input of bar codes into record					
Other (Specify and check status)					

Figure 5.1 (cont'd.)

CIRCULATION	OA	ONA	UD	PLANNED	EDA
Ability to maintain inventory control over all items in library or libraries					
Online check-in (charge)					
Online checkout (discharge)					
Online renewals					
Maintain record of item activity, no. of times circulated, etc.					
Place holds on items					
Overdues:					
Print notices					
Flag patron record					
Fines:					
Compute fines automatically					
Print fine notices to patrons					
Credit full or partial payment of fines					
Discharge paid fines on patron record					
Branches:					
Maintain circulation functions for branches					
Maintain circulation functions for multi-campus environment					
Maintain and report statistics:					
Patrons by category					
Items by subject category					
Items by format category					
Circle: Daily Monthly Annually					
Reserve room module					
Provision varying loan periods according to:					
Patron category					
Item format or type					
Provisions for a grace period (omit fine for first five days overdue)					
Capability of changing:					
Item records					
Patron records					
Fine amounts					
Input formats accepted. Indicate all					
Bar code					
OCR-A					
New ALS type font					
Other (specify)					

Figure 5.1 (cont'd.)

	OA	ONA	UD	PLANNED	EDA
CIRCULATION (CONTINUED)					
Cancellation of lost or stolen cards					
Displays:					
Books charged to patrons					
Requests by a patron					
Indicate item status in online public catalog:					
On shelf					
Checked out					
On cart					
Portable item (book) code reader for inventory and backup					
Automatic verification of patron eligibility					
Maximum number of patron categories?					
Maximum number of material categories?					
Maximum number of subject categories?					
Record bad check-ins on patron record					
Access to item records by:					
Call number					
Item code					
Author					
Title					
Access to patron records by:					
Patron code number					
Name					
Social security number					
Ability to print lists of :					
Missing items					
Overdues					
Other (specify and indicate status)					
ONLINE PUBLIC CATALOG					
Ability to search records by:					
Author					
Title					
Uniform title					
Added entries					
Subject heading					
Series					
By any MARC field or tag					
Boolean searches using operators:					
AND					
OR					
NOT					
to combine terms					
Other (specify and indicate status)					

Figure 5.1 (cont'd.)

	OA	ONA	UD	PLANNED	EDA
ONLINE PUBLIC CATALOG (CONTINUED)					
Instring searching, i.e. will find term regardless of location in the string or field searched, title for example ____					
"Full text" searching. Will find term regardless of where it is located in the record ____					
Browsing by:					
Author ____					
Subject ____					
Title ____					
Call number ____					
Indicate status of items displayed:					
On order ____					
In-process ____					
Available for circulation ____					
Checked-out ____					
On cart ____					
Branch or campus location ____					
Access via acoustical coupler RS232 using phone port ____					
Displays:					
Upper/lower case ____					
Abbreviated record ____					
Full record ____					
Partial record ____					
Other (specify and indicate status) ____					
Statistics on terminal activity					
No. of times used ____					
Type of use:					
Author ____					
Title ____					
Subject ____					
Other (specify indicate status) ____					
SERIALS					
Serials check-in ____					
Serials control, claiming ____					
Serials routing ____					
Bindery records ____					
Other (specify and indictate status) ____					

Figure 5.1 (cont'd.)

	OA	ONA	UD	PLANNED	EDA
ADMINISTRATION (MANAGEMENT INFORMATION SYSTEM)					
Throughput activity to monitor work flow (capture statistics on):					
Acquisitions					
Order price versus actual price					
Vendor data time lapse to fill orders					
No. of POs generated					
Cataloging					
Circulation					
New patron list					
New item list					
Summary data on items circulated by category					
Number of patrons					
Number of item codes					
Branch activity statistics					
Online public catalog					
Public catalog use statistics					
Serials					
Intra-library electronic message system to branches or campuses					
No. of system overrides					
Other (specify and indicate status)					

NATURE OF SYSTEM:
  Turnkey only (vendor modifications only)...
  Turnkey modifiable by institution under licensing
    agreement...
TYPE OF HARDWARE: IBM... DEC... HP... D G... OTHER...

Equipment is: Off-the-shelf unmodified...
         Modified equipment...
         Custom built...
Equipment compatible with:
  IBM DEC HP DG Other (specify)
PHONE PORTS: 300 baud... 1200 baud... 9600 baud...
TRAINING: At installation site...
       At vendor site also...
       Vendor site only...
NO. OF INSTALLATIONS BY TYPE:
    Academic libraries? _____
    Public Libraries? _____
    Government libaries (state and federal)? _____
    Special libraries (includes corporate)? _____

Figure 5.1 (cont'd.)

SPECIAL FEATURES OF SYSTEM   Specify.

PLEASE PROVIDE LIST OF INSTALLATIONS AND NAME AND ADDRESS OF KNOWN USERS GROUPS ON SEPARATE SHEET.

Please respond by no later than February 14, 1983.
Thank you for your cooperation.

RESPONDENT: _____

TITLE: _____

Please send completed survey to:

    David C. Genaway
    University Librarian
    Youngstown State University
    Youngstown, OH 44555

6

Profiles of Integrated Online Library Systems

This chapter offers a brief background and description of approximately 30 integrated online library systems available in the U.S., Canada and abroad as of spring 1984. The systems described in this chapter are those that operate on mainframes or minicomputers. Comprehensive data on more than 20 of these systems are summarized in Appendix A. Microcomputer-based systems are described in Chapter 7.

The reports on systems and vendors should not be taken to be all inclusive or exclusive, and the reader is strongly advised to check with vendors of interest for the latest information. (Addresses and telephone numbers for the vendors listed can be found in Appendix B.) The information in this chapter was derived from the author's survey, described in Chapter 5, personal interviews and vendor literature.

An approximate cost or cost range of the system software and/or hardware is given where available. The cost given is for outright purchase or license, unless otherwise noted. Readers should keep in mind that prices are extremely volatile because of rapidly changing hardware capabilities. Further, each library will have different specifications that will affect costs.

This author experienced a wide range of quotations when soliciting bids for a given library system with a stated number of terminals and printers. As stated elsewhere in this book, a great deal of effort is needed to establish a uniform basis for comparison of quotes, since many factors (maintenance costs, differences in subsystems' capabilities, etc.) will affect the final price of a system.

Several of the systems described in this chapter are not presently available in the United States. They have been included here because of library interest in them, and because it is likely that they will be introduced in the U.S. in the near future. When possible, at least one location of a U.S. installed system has been given. Contact individual vendors for the names of additional customers.

ADVANCED DATA MANAGEMENT (BIBLIOTECH)

BiblioTech is a software package developed by Advanced Data Management (ADM) and marketed by Comstow Information Services. Essentially two separate firms, there is a handshaking agreement between ADM and Comstow. Comstow is the marketing and user liaison firm, while ADM is the programming development organization.

ADM is a state-of-the-art software firm whose sole product is DRS, a database management system, and its applications packages, of which BiblioTech—the library system—is one. DRS has been used for special library management for more than 10 years, as well as for publishing applications since it was first installed in 1970. BiblioTech is described as having a complete and fully integrated library system. ADM provides all programming support and software systems design for BiblioTech.

Comstow Information Services is a library consulting firm, which specializes in research library system design and analysis, and does a wide variety of library automation work. Comstow provides the library expertise in the designing of BiblioTech by specifying the operations and functions the system must perform. Comstow is responsible for BiblioTech training manuals, instruction and user support. On-site training is available.

Functions and Description: Acquisitions, cataloging, circulation, online public access catalog, serials, browsing and authority maintenance. A fund accounting module is operational but not yet available.

BiblioTech can add or delete book records, analytics, journal articles and documents or reports to its online catalog. It can also provide keyword out of context (KWOC) indexes and conduct full-text Boolean searches. Browsing by index, short citation or full citation is provided. The circulation module can initiate recalls and accommodate holding (reserves).

All 88 record fields are accessible in BiblioTech's catalog mode. Bar code input can be developed, but "if circulation transactions are less than 25 a day, bar-coding all items would not be justified."[1] BiblioTech has clear menus but is not in MARC format or MARC-based. MARC tapes can be loaded, but an online OCLC interface is not available. Displays are in three levels in the browsing mode: index terms only with the number of hits after each, short citations or full citations. BiblioTech is screen-oriented and its multi-user configuration allows for partitioned databases for security purposes.

Installation is usually done by the purchaser's computer center. When the system is purchased, program tapes are mailed and the systems manager installs them. Many of the software capabilities are hardware dependent.

Equipment: Operates on DEC VAX and PDP 11 series.

Installations: Eight installations, primarily in corporate libraries.

Nature: Turnkey or software-only.

Price: Basic single user update mode is $15,000. Circulation and serials modes are $3000 each.

ADVANCED LIBRARY CONCEPTS (ADLIB)

This California-based firm is relatively new on the market and features a fairly complete selection of menu-driven modules.

Functions and Description: Acquisitions, AV materials booking, cataloging, circulation, fund accounting, online public access catalog and serials control. ADLIB also has "interlibrary loan" and reserve book room modules.

Equipment: Operates on IBM 4300, Digital Equipment Corp. (DEC), Honeywell, Altos and Prime computers, the IBM PC and equipment using the PICK operating system.

Installations: Being installed at University of Hawaii at Manoa as of summer 1984.

Nature: Modifiable turnkey.

Price: Software costs from $3000 to $95,000 and runs on equipment costing from $5000 to $900,000.

AMALGAMATED WIRELESS, LTD. (URICA)

At the time of this writing only limited data were available.

Functions and Description: Monographic acquisitions, cataloging, circulation and serials control. URICA's inquiry capability offers Boolean logic and an authority file.

Equipment: Operates on Microdata Reality 6000 or 8000, Sequel System VMS 3265 and equipment using the PICK operating system.

Installations: Six including college, university and municipal libraries.

Nature: Turnkey.

Price: Prices vary according to equipment configuration. Contact vendor.

AUREC INFORMATION & DIRECTORY SYSTEMS, LTD. (ALEPH)

ALEPH was developed by the Hebrew University in Jerusalem. Limited information was available at the time of this writing, but the system is described as having total integrated library services in one system.

Functions and Description: Acquisitions, free form cataloging, circulation, public catalog with browsing and Boolean operations, and serials check-in, control and claiming.

Equipment: Operates on DEC VAX.

Installations: Hebrew University.

Nature: Turnkey.

Price: Prices vary according to equipment configuration. Contact vendor.

AVATAR

OCLC, Inc. acquired Avatar in 1983. For information on the Avatar system, please see the discussion under OCLC, Inc.

BATTELLE (BASIS)

Battelle is an applied research laboratory founded in Columbus, OH, in 1929 with 30 people. Today it is a multinational organization with some 7500 scientists, engineers and economists whose training and skills embrace engineering, physics, and social and behavioral sciences. Battelle played a key role in developing the Universal Product Code symbol (bar code) used in supermarkets for product identification. Each year more than 2000 studies are conducted in engineering, manufacturing, transportation, national security and other areas.

Battelle has developed a data management system (DBMS) called BASIS. TECHLIB, the library system, is one part of BASIS. TECHLIB is limited to the library application. BASIS is a rather universal DMS capable of handling a wide variety of data (personnel, electronic file cabinets, litigation support, research applications, project management and library automation). The BASIS library package was introduced at the 1983 Special Libraries Association (SLA) meeting.

Functions and Description: Acquisitions, cataloging, circulation and online public access catalog both on-site and via dial-up access. A serials control module, which is operational but not yet available, will handle check-in, claiming, routing and ordering in a separate database. BASIS has a search/circulation system, document locator file, audio-visual inventory information, electronic card catalog and periodical index. A fund accounting module is being developed.

One of the most current applications of BASIS is the support of a newspaper library with a full-text retrieval system. It can use either bar codes or an optical scanner. The initial menu displays 16 choices identified by a capital letter. These options cover virtually every activity needed by either the public or librarians. Searches can be conducted using key words (for example, authors, titles, publishers or places) as well as subjects. Boolean operator search strategies can be used and availability queried. Books can be checked out/in and acquisition and cataloging records can be entered with a line by line inquiry.

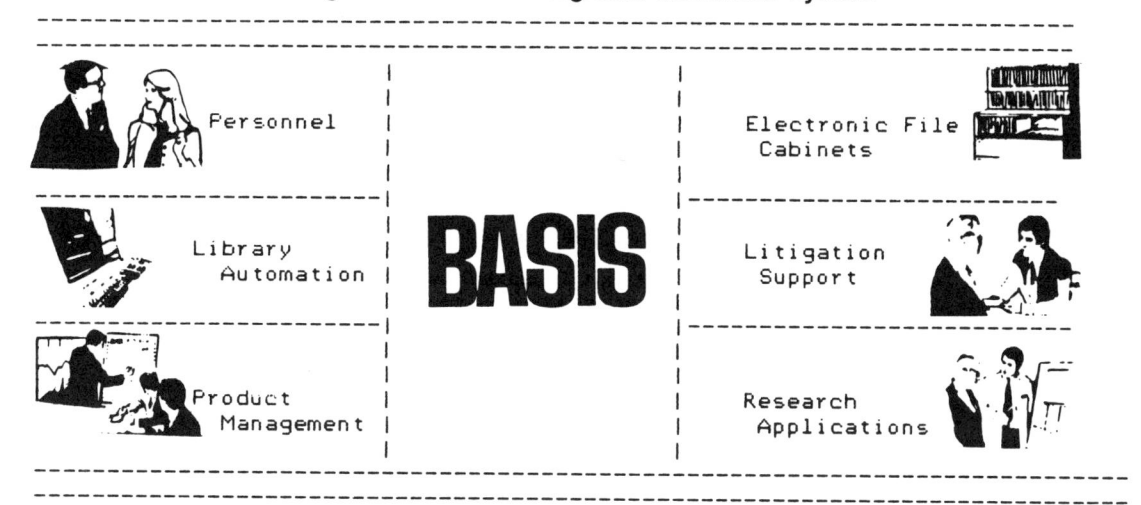

Figure 6.1: BASIS Integrated Institution System

- Personnel
- Library Automation
- Product Management
- BASIS
- Electronic File Cabinets
- Litigation Support
- Research Applications

Source: Battelle Research Laboratories. Reproduced with permission.

Interestingly, the system has not yet been installed in the laboratory's own research library which should be an ideal place to test it.

Battelle's Technical Advisory Group analyzes changing needs of libraries and information centers and suggests innovations. Documentation is provided as well as maintenance. Travel expenses for on-site support are not covered by Battelle.

Equipment: Operates on a wide variety of mainframe and minicomputers including IBM 370, IBM 4300 series, Control Data Corp. (CDC) Cyber and 6000, UNIVAC, DEC 10, DEC 20 and DEC VAX, and Wang VS.

Installations: Twelve special libraries.

Nature: Software-only.

Price: Computer software for the basic or central library system ranges from $37,000 for a minicomputer to $50,000 for a mainframe. Optional software modules range from $2000 to $15,000 each.

BIBLIOCENTRE DIVISION, CENTENNIAL COLLEGE (BIBLIOCENTRE)

The Bibliocentre Division of Centennial College (Canada) acquired DOBIS from the National Library of Canada and LIBIS from the University of Leuven, before IBM started marketing the system.[2] (See discussion under IBM, below.) Bibliocentre modified the software to suit its internal needs and started marketing it in response to interest from other libraries.

Functions and Description: The acquisitions and circulation subsystems have been revised and enhanced. The online public access catalog has remained essentially the same as the original DOBIS. The Bibliocentre system features a Datapack network for centralized processing and maintains a 1.6 million-record database of both Canadian and LC MARC format records. Bibliocentre extends online ordering and circulation to its clients.

Equipment: Operates on IBM 33 computers.

Installations: There are 20 colleges in 120 locations using this software in either a dial-up or stand-alone mode.

Nature: Software-only. (Bibliocentre will assist in selecting hardware.)

Price: The price of software including installation and training is $100,000. The price is dependent on present record format. It does not include data conversion of all records.

BIBLIO-TECHNIQUES, INC. (BLIS)

The Biblio-Techniques Library and Information System (BLIS) software is based on the Washington Library Network (WLN) software. It can be purchased independently or together with hardware.

Functions and Description: Acquisitions, cataloging, fund accounting and online public access catalog. A circulation module is under development and serials control is planned. It supports monographs, serials, microforms and non-print media MARC formats. The authority control file has linked bibliographic records and automatic verification. BLIS is MARC-based and contains full MARC records. Its online public access catalog allows Boolean operator searches on keywords or specified data fields.

The system has several screens of definitions of terms and provides keyword or term searching. Help screens are available. There are two levels of bibliographic displays: one for first time users and one for experienced users. The online catalog module lets patrons select the mode of searching: tutorial or command. If a Telex 479 terminal is used with the system, data can be presented in three colors (blue, green and red). Screens are custom tailored to meet the needs of each library.

Equipment: Operates on Magnuson M80/42 CPU. Linkage with the MELVYN system is planned through an interface. Hardware and software are compatible with an IBM mainframe or an AG DataBase Machine mainframe. The CPU should have a minimum of 1MB (mega or million bytes). The operating systems are MVS or VS and the programming languages are COM-PLEAT and ADABASE/WLN.

Installations: At least seven installations including the University of California at San Diego, Columbia University, Johns Hopkins University and several Australian institutions.

Nature: Turnkey or software-only.

Price: Software-only ranges from $165,000 to $240,000.

CALS SERVICE GROUP, LTD. (CALS)

The Comprehensive Automated Learning Resources System (CALS) is described as a "comprehensive automated system for libraries and media centers. . . . Designed within a community college environment to meet the needs of small- and medium-sized colleges, it is also appropriate for school and public libraries." It accommodates media and audiovisual formats. This system offers automated conversion from OCLC or MARC tapes, custom conversion from an existing automated file, full online data entry and abbreviated data entry for immediate circulation.

Functions and Description: Acquisitions, AV materials booking, circulation and online public access catalog. It includes daily equipment delivery and equipment usage reports in addition to conventional circulation functions, scheduling, serials holdings, acquisitions, MARC record conversion program, art slide retrieval by descriptor list, and bibliographic and patron control. A serials control subsystem is under development and fund accounting is planned.

CALS uses standard IBM support products, such as the DL/1 database management system and CICS telecommunications. The system uses COBOL language and is table-driven from a set of policies and procedures. OCR-A format is both human and machine-readable. In the online catalog module, a phonetic algorithm allows successful retrieval in spite of punctuation errors, common misspellings or truncation.

Equipment: Operates on IBM equipment.

Installations: Elgin Community College and Illinois Valley Community College of Oglesby.

Nature: Software-only.

Price: Approximately $30,000.

CARLYLE SYSTEMS, INC., (TOMUS)

Based loosely on MELVYL, the University of California's online union catalog, The Online Multiple User System (TOMUS) is being marketed through regional library networks.

Functions and Description: Online public access catalog. Cataloging and circulation modules are under development. An interface has been developed that allows you to use the INNOVACQ software for acquisitions and serials control. TOMUS supports monographs, serials, microforms and maps MARC formats. Standard search procedures, keyword or term searching, and Boolean operators (AND, OR, NOT) are supported. Word stems can be used as search terms and search results can be narrowed or expanded by modifiers. Help screens are available. The patron can select the mode for searching (tutorial/command). TOMUS can be used to generate a COM catalog which can serve as a backup. It has four-level bibliographic record displays.[4]

Terminals in customer libraries are hooked up through dedicated lines to a computer center operated by Carlyle Systems, within a specific geographic area. Local area network (LAN) capability promotes local resource sharing.

There are 16 models of Carlyle computers and a Carlyle custom chip has been developed.

Equipment: Hardware is IBM compatible and operates on two Magnuson M80132 mainframe CPUs with 8MB each. The operating system is OS/360 (modified) Assembly. The programming language is SPITBALL.

Installations: Four academic libraries, one public library in New York state, one special library, New York Public Library Research Library and San Francisco Public Library.

Nature: Software-only or turnkey.

Price: Prices vary according to equipment configuration. Contact vendor.

C L SYSTEMS, INC. (LIBS 100)

C L Systems, Inc. (CLSI) is one of the largest turnkey vendors of integrated online library systems. It has the most installations. The LIBS 100 was developed in 1971 to provide automated products and services to libraries.[5] The initial LIBS 100 system was used for book acquisitions, and first became operational in spring 1972 at the Cleveland Public Library. The first circulation control application was in the Marin County (CA) Public Library in December 1974.

In 1982 the first CLSI libraries began loading MARC II records. Some new innovations include a microcomputer system (described in Chapter 7), DataLink, which allows access to five online databases via Dialog, and a MARC editing terminal.

Preinstallation requirements are well defined and one of the most comprehensive manuals on site preparation and environmental requirements has been prepared by CLSI. The company claims 98% up time for the system. CLSI has flexible arrangements for purchasing, and continually updates and enhances its software. There have been more than 26 releases or upgraded versions to date. CLSI's Customer Service Organization and Systems Support Group (SSG) provide immediate telephone assistance seven days a week. The SSG assists in problem and isolation diagnosis, and has offices throughout the U.S. and Canada.

Although CLSI's age, experience and size are advantages, they may eventually prove to be drawbacks. The ability to maintain innovation and responsiveness in spite of the company's size will require a continuing conscious effort by CLSI's management.

Functions and Description: Acquisitions, AV materials booking, cataloging, circulation, fund accounting, online public access catalogs with authority control, Boolean search capability, and reserve book room. A serials control module is planned. Interfaces include OCLC, RLIN, UTLAS, WLN and MINIMARC.

Current input/output limitations that have an upper limit of about 250 terminals due to the unibus architecture will be lifted by new system architecture which is currently under development.

Equipment: All equipment is marketed as CL Systems, but the system operates on DEC micro and minicomputers, CDC disk drives and Lear Seigler terminals. A laser scanner which is used for checkouts is a unique feature. It is rapid and easy to use and eliminates problems sometimes associated with bar code reading wands. The touch terminal, though quite expensive as of spring 1984 ($5000), is unique.

Installations: As of early 1984, CLSI had 220 central installations serving 600 libraries, including 12 in Australia and two in the Netherlands. U.S. installations include Providence Public Library, Baltimore County Public Library, Carnegie-Stout (IA) Public Library, College of DuPage Learning Resource Center and Memphis State University Library.

Nature: Turnkey (libraries are sometimes allowed to purchase terminals independently).

Price: Prices begin at $70,000 for the PDP 11/23 microcomputer system (including hardware and software) and go up depending on system requirements.

DATA PHASE SYSTEMS, INC. (ALIS)

Data Phase was founded in 1975 to develop and implement customized approaches to inventory control, order entry and distributed data collection. Data Phase is staffed by more than 60 employees, a number of whom have either library degrees or some library experience, with 40% of them involved in developmental activities. The president of Data Phase was formerly vice president of Western Union, where he was responsible for Western Union's electronic mail product.

At its inception, Data Phase entered the library industry with bar code and OCR techniques. After a comprehensive year-long study of public and academic library needs and existing automated capabilities, it developed a total information system, the Automated Library Information System (ALIS). It was based on a pilot project called Automated Information Resources System (AIRS), developed by Data Phase for the Dallas County Community College District in 1977. AIRS was one of the first successful integrated library systems. It originated on the District's library system which never had a card catalog but was based on a machine-readable database that had existed since 1965.

Early in 1983 the newly formed Connecticut Consortium Libraries On Line (LION) consisting of both academic and public libraries began providing a full MARC database for the development of extensive bibliographic files using the Data Phase System.[7]

Functions and Description: Acquisitions, cataloging, circulation, fund accounting, online public access catalog (author, title search available and subject search and call number search in beta test, the final testing project just prior to marketing), materials and film booking (a pilot project in the testing stage), reserve book room, COM support and technical services. The acquisitions subsystem contains several files: fund file, supplier file and selection list file. The acquisitions file contains one acquisition record for every title requested, ordered, received, claimed, in-process, etc., and is also accessible in the full ALIS database. A serials control module is planned.

Equipment: Operates on Data General and Tandem computers.

Installations: More than 60, including 11 multi-library systems and more than 24 academic libraries.

Nature: Turnkey.

Price: Prices vary according to system requirements. Approximate price for a library with 400,000 titles, an annual circulation of 120,000 and 30,000 patrons was $270,000 in 1983. The system requires several different licensing and/or service agreements.

DATA RESEARCH ASSOCIATES, INC. (ATLAS)

Incorporated in 1975 to provide data processing systems and services to libraries and small businesses, Data Research Associates (DRA) began services to libraries in 1976. The system is commonly referred to as DRA, yet the system is officially called A Total Automated Library System (ATLAS). DRA's initial involvement was in developing automated systems for libraries for the blind and physically handicapped, including the Library for the Blind and Physically Handicapped in St. Louis. Some of DRA's earlier projects were a newspaper indexing package and the preliminary design for a Union List of serials. In the past three years it has entered the general library automation market with its MARC database management software and circulation software.

According to the vendor, DRA provides " . . . a complete MARC record with total editing capability. Any field, subfield, tag or indicator may be edited without changing the entire record or the order of the fields. Bibliographic data are entered and stored once only. It can handle multiple agencies and inter- and intra-library loan."

Although source codes will not be supplied directly to the user, they will be placed in an escrow account in the event that DRA should ever cease to do business.

Functions and Description: Acquisitions, AV materials booking, cataloging, circulation, fund accounting, online public access catalog and some parts of serials control (ordering and check-in) are operational. Two screen formats are available for bibliographic records: partial and full MARC. DRA's experience with the materials for the blind has provided a strong materials booking system. It has a well developed acquisitions subsystem which includes: analysis and support of collection development, pre-order searching, title under consideration processing, subscription control, purchase order processing, materials receipt processing, management of memberships, exchange partnerships and contributions, some of which are closely integrated with other library system modules, such as the public access catalog.

The system uses the standardized accounting software Digital Integrated Business System (DIBS). There are six main files in the acquisitions subsystem: titles database, program control and constant data file, organization master file, materials acquisitions file, purchase order file and account master file. It has a Union List of Periodicals module and generates several useful management reports including a list of titles that have not circulated since a given date.

Equipment: Operates on DEC or Digital's VAX computers.

Installations: Twenty-one libraries for the blind and physically handicapped, three academic libraries, three government libraries, one special library and one public library. The first public library system was introduced at the Cleveland Public Library in 1983. It took DRA more than two years to develop this system, but it anticipates that systems can be up much faster now that the initial development stage is over.[6]

Nature: Turnkey.

Price: Depending on the number of terminals, etc., approximately $240,000 to $440,000 based on a medium-sized library containing 400,000 titles and having an annual circulation of 120,000.

ELECTRIC MEMORY, INC. (EMILS/3000)

As of this writing, Electric Memory's EMILS/3000 IOLS was still undergoing "beta" site testing at Chabot College (CA), where it is being refined.

Functions and Description: Circulation, online public access catalog and database control. Acquisitions, AV materials booking and serials modules are under development. A technical literature management capability is also under development.

EMILS/3000 features inverse display to highlight fields and function keys. Vendor literature reports that the system "allows many different modules to access a single bibliographic record with multiple indexes." A maximum of 250 terminals can be networked to one system and multiple systems can be linked. The system uses a microcomputer for data conversion. The system is described as accommodating 2 million circulation transactions of 700,000 items annually.

Equipment: Operates on Hewlett-Packard 3000 series equipment.

Installations: One academic library, Chabot College (Hayword, CA). It is being installed at the Logan Public (UT) Library.

Nature: Turnkey or software-only.

Price: The database control module, the circulation system and online catalog combined cost approximately $64,500. There will be an annual update fee of 10% of the module cost which includes a hotline service. Hardware costs were estimated to be $140,000 to $610,000 in 1983.[8] There is a one-time software license fee that includes installation, documentation and training.

GEAC LTD. (GEAC LIBRARY INFORMATION SYSTEM/GLIS)

A Canadian-based firm with offices in the U.S., England and Germany, Geac manufactures computers, and programs them for online systems in banking, pharmacy and library operations. Geac was founded in 1971 by R.A. German and R.K. Isserstedt. Of 15 managers and employees profiled in Geac's literature, almost all have electrical engineering, programming or corporate management backgrounds. Although there are librarians on the staff, none were clearly identified as such in the corporate sketches.

The Geac 8000, introduced in 1977, was designed to handle large numbers of terminals accessing large databases. Geac's philosophy is to provide customers with a solution to computing needs at a known cost. Quotations are usually in the currency of the requesting country. Geac manufactures its own equipment instead of using off-the-shelf equipment of other vendors. The number of Geac installations is growing substantially. With annual revenues in excess of $30 million, it is among the largest corporations in the integrated library system market. However, only $11 million was generated from the sale of library systems in 1982.[9]

Functions and Description: Acquisitions, AV materials booking, cataloging, circulation, fund accounting, online public access catalog and serials control. Basic services include systems analysis, hardware, applications software, maintenance of hardware and software, and full facilities management. Data compression techniques allow storage of large amounts of data in a given amount of disk space. OCLC, RLIN, UTLAS, tape and MINIMARC interfaces are available.

Faxon and Geac are working on an interface to link the Geac integrated library system with Faxon's LINX network for online searching, tape exchange and communications. Online access to LINX network files and databases, use of the LINX COURIER electronic mail system for both users, the ability to transfer holding from LINX to Geac and invoicing information are also being developed.

Equipment: Geac manufactures and uses most of its own computer equipment, in conjunction with CDC disk drives and Kennedy tape drives.

Installations: More than 70 libraries including academic, public, consortia, etc. Ten Geac systems are installed in England and one in the Netherlands. The Smithsonian Library has contracted with Geac to install a system in its main library and 15 branch libraries throughout the Washington, DC area as well as in Arizona, New York City and the Republic of Panama. The system will include a MARC record management system in addition to most other modules. A total of 190 terminals is planned.

Nature: Turnkey.

Price: Approximate price for a library with 400,000 titles, 120,000 circulation transactions and 30,000 patrons per year was $340,000 in 1983.

GEORGETOWN UNIVERSITY MEDICAL CENTER (LIS)

The LIS (Library Information System) is another one of the medical library family of integrated library systems. It is based on NLM's ILS (integrated library system) but it has a more general application. LIS was designed and implemented at the Dahlgren Library of the Georgetown University Medical Center in 1980 to 1981.

Georgetown will assist in software installation, defining the system parameters and training and documentation. It will also provide software for file conversion and the loading of machine-readable tapes. Computer-assisted instruction is provided through Georgetown's QUEST software. The contracting library pays for travel expenses when Georgetown personnel are required for on-site maintenance. Phone consultation is provided for a monthly fee to include up to eight non-cumulative hours of problem diagnosis and resolution. Enhancements are made available as part of Georgetown's service contract.

Functions and Description: Acquisitions, cataloging, circulation, online public access catalog, serials control, accounting/word processing, mini-MEDLINE system and networking.

The acquisitions subsystem maintains all orders and fiscal records online and generates purchase orders. Special management reports provide information on collection development. Order status is available through the online public access catalog.

Serials control interfaces with PHILSOM III, the medical network for serials, which allows access by truncated keywords or title and ISSN number. Holdings are current to the minute.

Mini-MEDLINE includes special software which allows users to conduct searches on a subset of MEDLINE citations, referencing journals held by the library. This subsystem is more useful to clinical medicine staff than to in-depth researchers. The authority control for LIS is obtained from the medical library subject heading list.

The system is programmed in ANSI standard MUMPS using the ISM-11 Operating System. With a baud rate of 9600, screen displays and responses are almost instantaneous. Three levels of records are maintained: the comprehensive MARC record for catalogers, an abbreviated three-line display for users and a full display that replicates a standard card and contains call number, full bibliographic description and tracings.

By filing an electronic form at the public catalog terminal, patrons can request interlibrary loans. A local area network that includes electronic mail and access to patient information is planned. Additional modules will be available as separately priced options.

Equipment: Operates on Plessey Peripheral Systems or DEC equipment. A microcomputer option that can include the full system for small libraries operates on the Motorola Model 68 microprocessor (see Chapter 7).

Installations: The University of Texas Health Science Center at San Antonio, which has 27 terminals operational.

Nature: Software-only.

Price: $30,000 to $65,000 depending on the equipment configuration used.

IBM

DOBIS/LIBIS

IBM, under contract to the Dortmund Library System in Germany and the Leuven Library System in Belgium, developed an automated library system called DOBIS/LIBIS, to provide an interactive online library system combining all repetitive records and operations.[10] It was designed as a "total online library system," including acquisitions, cataloging, circulation, serials and catalog search.

The Leuven Library System-Online was originally developed by the University of Leuven in Belgium. The Dortmund Library System was developed by the University of Dortmund and serves as the base for the Leuven Library System-Batch and the Leuven Library System. In 1976, the National Library of Canada signed a contract with the University of Dortmund for DOBIS, whereupon Dortmund arranged for IBM to convert the cataloging and search modules. The work was performed by an American couple, Caryl and Stratton McAllister, working for IBM in Stuttgart, Germany. Later, the University of Leuven signed a contract for the rewrite of the acquisitions and circulation modules. IBM subsequently made an agreement with the University of Dortmund for marketing rights to its cataloging and catalog search modules and another with the University of Leuven for marketing rights to the acquisitions and circulation modules.[11]

The combined DOBIS/LIBIS (Dortmunder Bibliothekssystem/Leuvens Integral Bibliothek System) is one of the earliest systems with MARC-compatible records that had most of the major subsystems of a library operational, and was designed for all types of libraries.

Today, ongoing maintenance is virtually nil and IBM must be prodded to obtain details on the system or even to sell it. For support one must rely on the original purchasers of the system who have had the most experience with it. IBM announced that there would be no more support for the system after February 1983. The latest release of LIBIS-

Batch is 1.0 with no error correction devices. (See also Bibliocentre Division Centennial College for updated version.)

Libraries purchasing library applications software from IBM should get written commitments with regard to future product support. This is in light of recent announcements that IBM has developed a series of new modules for the North American version of DOBIS. The new features include Boolean search capabilities and "help" modules, a periodicals control system, online entry for full-text abstracts and batch programs for statistical analysis of management information.[13] IBM does not plan to make a new release of DOBIS/LIBIS available in the U.S., but a new release was made available outside of the U.S. and is described, below, under IBM DOBIS-SSX/VSE.

The *Installed User Program: Librarian's Guide,* outlining the basic functions with sample screen menus, is available from IBM.[12]

Functions and Description: Acquisitions, cataloging, circulation, serials and catalog searching.

Equipment: Operates on IBM computers.

Installations: Ryerson Polytechnic was the first user of DOBIS/LIBIS in North America, having obtained the system from IBM-Canada. There are presently licenses for the system in Israel, Italy, Japan, South Africa and France.

Nature: Turnkey.

Price: Prices vary depending on equipment configuration. Contact vendor.

Nature: Software and hardware purchased independently.

Price: Acquiring the system is unique. The software is rented from IBM as an "Installed User Package" for two years for approximately $2000 a month. After the 24-month period, the monthly charges are waived, and the user has a paid-up license. Specific price information is available from local IBM representatives.

DOBIS/LIBIS-SSX/VSE

The IBM DOBIS/LIBIS-SSX/VSE is a newer version of the DOBIS/LIBIS system described above. It is an online library management system that handles all the activities of libraries, document collections and archives. Self-installation of the system is reported to be easy through SSX/VSE (Small System Executive/Virtual System Extended). Sample problems are included to test major functions. All online functions are tailored to a library's needs. The "Librarian's Guide" and "Installation and Operations Guide" are very detailed. At present, the system is not available in the U.S.

Functions and Description: Includes acquisitions with financial control and follow-up of orders, cataloging, public access catalog, periodicals control including claiming, networking, statistical management information and circulation.

Equipment: IBM 4300 Processor supported by SSX/VSE.

Nature: Turnkey.

Price: Contact IBM Stuttgart for license agreements.

LIPMAN MANAGEMENT RESOURCES, LTD. (ADLIB)

Lipman Management Resources is based in Berkshire, England. Currently, ADLIB (ADaptive LIBrary management system) is not available in the U.S. A more than 100-page ADLIB design manual is available from the manufacturer which describes the system in detail.

Functions and Description: Acquisitions, claiming, loan control, and controlled vocabulary and thesaurus management. The basic module can create and maintain databases. Free-text searching can be conducted using Boolean operators, including "greater than" and "less than." ADLIB handles collections of a non-bibliographic nature, such as artifacts and art museum holdings.

There is a special program which recognizes full MARC. Originally developed for U.K. MARC, a "full range of international MARC conventions will eventually be available." A MARC record is converted to ADLIB format and can be reconverted back to MARC format when records are exported.

The broader database system, of which ADLIB is a part, includes payroll, accounting, production control, job costing, budgeting systems, etc.

Equipment: Operates on a Prime 32-bit super minicomputer.

Nature: Turnkey.

Price: Prices vary according to equipment configuration. Contact vendor.

M/A-COM SIGMA DATA, INC. (DATALIB)

DATALIB, developed in 1978, is the IOLS offered by M/A-COM. Sigma Data was acquired by M/A-COM in late 1981. Until recently it has had a low profile and little market initiative.

M/A-Com stresses customized library service. Its literature states that "customization in the DATALIB context entails the selection of modules that will be included in the system; the definition of associated databases, including record types, data elements, searchable data elements, prompts, print names, authority files and stop-word lists; design of customized reports and forms; creation of the library codes that will allow the individual libraries within an agency to enter, retrieve and print reports showing their own data; and the establishment of authorizations which govern the modules, functions, library codes, record types and specific data elements to which each user has access."[14]

Functions and Description: Acquisitions, AV materials booking, cataloging, circulation, fund accounting, online public access catalog, copyrighting and an OCLC module. A serials control module is under development.

The accounting module cannot be purchased separately from the acquisitions module. The cataloging module has an associated user-defined authority file that instantly validates authority items in bibliographic records. Printed and COM catalogs can be produced.

Presently the circulation module requires keying in each transaction. Bar code input is under development. Temporary or ephemeral records can be created such as uncataloged materials or vertical file materials. A special copyright module records each instance of copying and the fees owed to various publishers can be calculated to generate publisher payment reports. The OCLC module offers the capability to convert and process archival records from tape and will allow direct interface with OCLC using a microprocessor.

DATALIB tracks and retrieves up to 25 different types of materials including contracts and press releases as well as books. These 25 different types of records can be searched simultaneously using the AND, OR, NOT and ADJACENT operators.

DATALIB supports multiple users, Boolean searching with up to 10 levels of nesting, free-text searching and uses of variable length records. MARC format records can be transferred into the database either through an interface or from tapes. MARC format is not retained as the record is reformatted. The system supports online and batch updating.

Equipment: Operates on DEC VAX and Data General minicomputers.

Installations: Fifteen corporate and government installations, including Schlumberger-Doll Research Library and the GM Tech Center Library.

Nature: Turnkey or software-only.

Price: The system is available through licensing, leasing or timesharing. Initial license, with all modules except OCLC interface and autodial, is $75,000.

NATIONAL LIBRARY OF MEDICINE (ILS)

The Integrated Library System (ILS) was originally developed at the Lister Hill Center for Biomedical Communications of the National Library of Medicine (NLM). It was initiated in 1977 as a research and development project which aimed to design a fully integrated minicomputer-based system—a system designed to support all library activities with one master file.

Beginning in 1977, NLM entered into an interagency agreement with the Army Library, Pentagon, in which the Army Library offered to serve as the ILS development and test site. System functions were developed throughout 1978-1979 at this library and in April 1980 the first version of the system was installed for Pentagon Library use.

The first version of ILS (ILS 1.0) included the circulation subsystem, a serials check-in module and routing slip printing capability. In summer 1980, it was made available for release in the public domain through the National Technical Information Service (NTIS), at a cost of $2000. The second release, version 2.0, was made available to NTIS for distribution in summer 1981. This version contained an online catalog, authority files and a more complete circulation subsystem.

Enhanced versions of ILS software were developed by two companies: Avatar Systems, Inc. and Online Computer Systems, Inc. Principals of both companies were heavily involved in the development of ILS at NLM and at the Pentagon Library. Until recently, the NLM ILS system has been supported by Online Computer Systems, Inc. Avatar updated and maintained service on its enhanced version of the system, and provided custom enhancements for its customers. In December 1983, Avatar was acquired by OCLC, Inc. Also in 1983, OCLC entered into a joint agreement with Online Computer Systems to market the LS/2000, an integrated system based on the ILS. (Avatar and Online Computer Systems are discussed in further detail in this chapter, under "OCLC, Inc.")

The NLM version of ILS is still available from NTIS for approximately $5700. A user manual for the NLM ILS can also be obtained from NTIS for a modest price.[15] Libraries with NLM's ILS have recently been worried about having support for their system or being "abandoned," since Avatar and Online Computer Systems have linked up with OCLC. In December 1983, Avatar indicated that negotiations with OCLC were to include support of existing Avatar systems. Online Computer Systems indicated that any future enhancements would have to be contracted with OCLC.[16] As of January 1984, NLM ceased further development of the ILS software.[17]

The general design criteria for the ILS are:

- Modular integration of functions and files;
- Operation on a range of hardware affordable by a wide range of libraries;
- Transportability/maintainability of programs;
- Multi-level user interface; and
- System network access.[18]

"Modular integration" is a design and implementation approach in which the functions of an integrated system may be developed as independent modules. Hence, all functions (or modules) do not have to be implemented on one computer. A modular design offers the greatest flexibility and extensibility over the life of the system. The system must ensure proper integration of subsequently developed modules. The objective is a design that would allow for distributed processing. For example, libraries that have heavy circulation and cataloging loads must be able to implement those functions on separate processors and still maintain access to a common Master Bibliographic File (MBF).

Based on the assumption that each class of user has his/her own interface requirements, and that no one interface can be equally effective for all, a multi-level user cordial interface was developed. Such different levels recognize the varying degrees of sophistication with which users approach the system (catalog librarians, subject specialists, etc.).

ILS is MARC-based and supports a fully MARC-compatible format. The MBF allows the librarian to be selective and to identify online which MARC tags and subfields are to be included in the MBF record when it is loaded into the MBF. The system is compatible with MEDLARS III.

Functions and Description: Supports bibliographic control, catalog access, circulation, serials control and administrative reports.

Searches can be conducted by author, title, subject, corporate and conference name, call number, unique ID such as ISBN, LC card number, OCLC number, and title key and author key searches with the 3,2,2,1 or 4,4 construction. Once hits have been found the user can browse for other titles, subjects or the like in the same alphabetical area.[19]

Equipment: Operates on Data General and DEC computers.

Installations: More than 12 private, government, medical and academic libraries, including Air Force Library (Maxwell Air Force Base) and East Carolina University (Greenville, NC).

Nature: Software-only.

Price: Program tape available from NTIS for $5700. Must also acquire MIIS (Meditech Interpretive Information System) license (approximately $8000) plus MUMPS language (estimated cost is $10,000 to $15,000). Operates on equipment costing from $25,000 to $50,000.

NORTHWESTERN UNIVERSITY (NOTIS)

Northwestern University was one of the earliest pioneers in automation. The NOTIS system began in 1967 and is now in its third generation. NOTIS has been in continuous use in the Northwestern University Library since 1970 and was installed at the Biblioteca National in 1979. In April 1983 the system was made available to libraries as an integrated library system.

NOTIS is an operationally tested set of computer programs with full documentation and procedures manuals. Northwestern has a separate information systems development office consisting of a director, systems engineer and professional librarian.

Functions and Description: Acquisitions, cataloging, circulation, fund accounting, online public access catalog and serials control. A revised circulation module is operational but not available.

NOTIS has a "self-service, online circulation system . . . which enables users to check-out their own material."[20] Report writer packages can be used to generate management statistics. The system accepts input from bar-coded labels, OCR labels, magnetic strips or punched cards. Source codes are included with instructions in a standard language. Since the system was installed in Venezuela, it is capable of handling Spanish language materials. Multi-level user guides are planned. Maintenance includes enhancements to programs as developed and assistance in installation and use of the system.

Equipment: Operates on IBM 5666-276 SSX/VSE PL-1 and on IBM compatible equipment using standard programming languages.

Installations: 10 academic libraries and one public library including the Evanston/Chicago Campus Library and the Biblioteca National in Venezuela.

Nature: Software-only.

Price: Pricing structure for software is $20,000 to $26,000 for an annual license fee or $65,000 to $90,000 for a permanent license fee, depending on the operating system and equipment configuration used.

OCLC, INC. (LS/2000)

OCLC, Inc. markets the LS/2000 integrated system, based on the ILS package developed at NLM. In 1983, OCLC purchased AVATAR and hired Richard S. Dick, president of AVATAR, to further develop the OCLC system. It also contracted with Online Computer Systems (OCS) to enhance the software to OCLC specifications and to support user clusters. (Both companies are discussed below.) Since the public domain, or NLM version, of ILS will receive no further government support for enhancements, the vendor support represented by AVATAR and OCS becomes more critical.

Another OCLC product, the Total Library System (TLS), based on the IOLS developed by Claremont College, is currently being marketed by OCLC in a revised format, primarily to special libraries.

Functions and Description: Circulation (including "cart control"), online public access catalog, serials control, authority file control function, catalog review function, online help subsystem and an administrative segment for defining policies and parameters. OCLC also has an acquisitions subsystem which is not a part of the LS/2000. At present, there is no compatibility for interchange of data between the acquisitions subsystem and the LS/2000. AV materials booking and fund accounting subsystems are planned.

Equipment: Operates on Data General equipment.

Installations: The first LS/2000 was installed in 1983 at the "Dublin Cluster" (University of Akron, Ohio Wesleyan University, Hampshire College and the OCLC Corporate Library) and for Five Colleges, Inc. (Amherst College, Hampshire College, Mount

Holyoke College, Smith College and the University of Massachusetts). It will be installed at the University of Newcastle in the United Kingdom.

Nature: Turnkey.

Price: Approximate price for a library with 400,000 titles, 120,000 annual circulation and 30,000 patrons was $290,000 in 1983. The maintenance costs for the system are higher than the average costs of most other systems surveyed.

Avatar

Avatar's major product has been a revised and enhanced version of the National Library of Medicine's (NLM's) Integrated Library System (ILS). It also conducted feasibility studies, assisted purchasers in the procurement and installation of hardware and software, tailored software to local needs and provided training. The system is no longer offered by Avatar, since the company has been purchased by OCLC. However, information on it has been included here because of the number of Avatar systems already in place in libraries, and because of the system's relationship to the LS/2000. Any inquiries regarding Avatar should be directed to OCLC.

Functions: Cataloging, circulation and online public access subsystems. Management statistics include circulation and database management activity. Reports by patron type and by item classification were under development. The Master Bibliographic File (MBF) accepts OCLC/RLIN MARC records directly from tape or direct OCLC interface converting pre-AACR2 records to AACR2 during the formatting process.

Equipment: Operates on DEC and Data General computers. Runs most efficiently on Data General equipment.

Installations: There are seven installations (three special libraries, two government libraries, one academic and one public library), including Carnegie-Mellon.

Nature: Turnkey. Software was also available independently. Contact OCLC for details.

Price: Contact vendor (OCLC). With this system, as with several others, there are three contractual and licensing agreements that must be signed: the NLM/NTIS license, the Avatar Program License Agreement and the MIIS computer program. This is typical of other systems emerging from the NLM/ILS program.

Online Computer Systems, Inc.

As noted earlier, Online Computer Systems (OCS) is the other vendor involved with NLM's ILS. OCS did not sell software; it sold the hardware, operating system, installation, initialization, training services, and ongoing maintenance and support. As a result of its arrangement with OCLC, OCS will now market the LS/2000 for OCLC. Any questions regarding enhancements to the NLM ILS software should be directed to OCLC. Again, information on the OCS version of ILS is provided below to give readers some background on the system.

Functions and Description: Circulation, cataloging and online public access. The authority control file must be established locally and is linked to bibliographic records. Keyword or term searching using Boolean operators (AND, OR, NOT) is available.[21] Supports MARC format.

Equipment: Operates on DEC and Data General computers and IBM minicomputers. The programming languages are MIIS/MUMPS.

Nature: Turnkey.

Price: The smallest two-terminal system started at under $50,000 in 1983. Contact vendor (OCLC).

ONLINE COMPUTER SYSTEMS, INC. (ILS)

Online Computer Systems entered into an agreement with OCLC in 1983. For information on this company, please see the discussion, above, under OCLC, Inc.

PENNSYLVANIA STATE UNIVERSITY (LIAS)

LIAS is being developed at Pennsylvania State University to meet the special needs of the university. It is designed to be a fully integrated information network that will be accessible through the various state campuses. (See Figure 6.2.)

Functions and Description: Cataloging, circulation, online public access catalog, COM and interlibrary loan support to 19 branch campuses throughout the state from the main University Park campus. Acquisitions and accounting modules are under development as well as a linkage with Faxon's LINX system. An interface to RLIN is operational and available, and linkages to BRS, DIALOG, Orbit and OCLC will be supported. Circulation uses bar-coded labels. The online public access catalog uses only a limited number of commands. Authority control, which will direct users to the required information rather than refer them to another term, is under development.

Key features are the ability to perform multiple library functions from any terminal; decentralized and multifaceted bibliographic access to all library resources by traditional access; search queries using free-form, natural language and keyword strategies with freedom from dependency on choice or form of access, filing order or word order; access to online commercial databases; "Selin" spine and item label preparation; bibliographies and text word processing.[22]

Equipment: Operates on a Honeywell mainframe.

Profiles of Integrated Online Library Systems 103

Figure 6.2: LIAS System Diagram

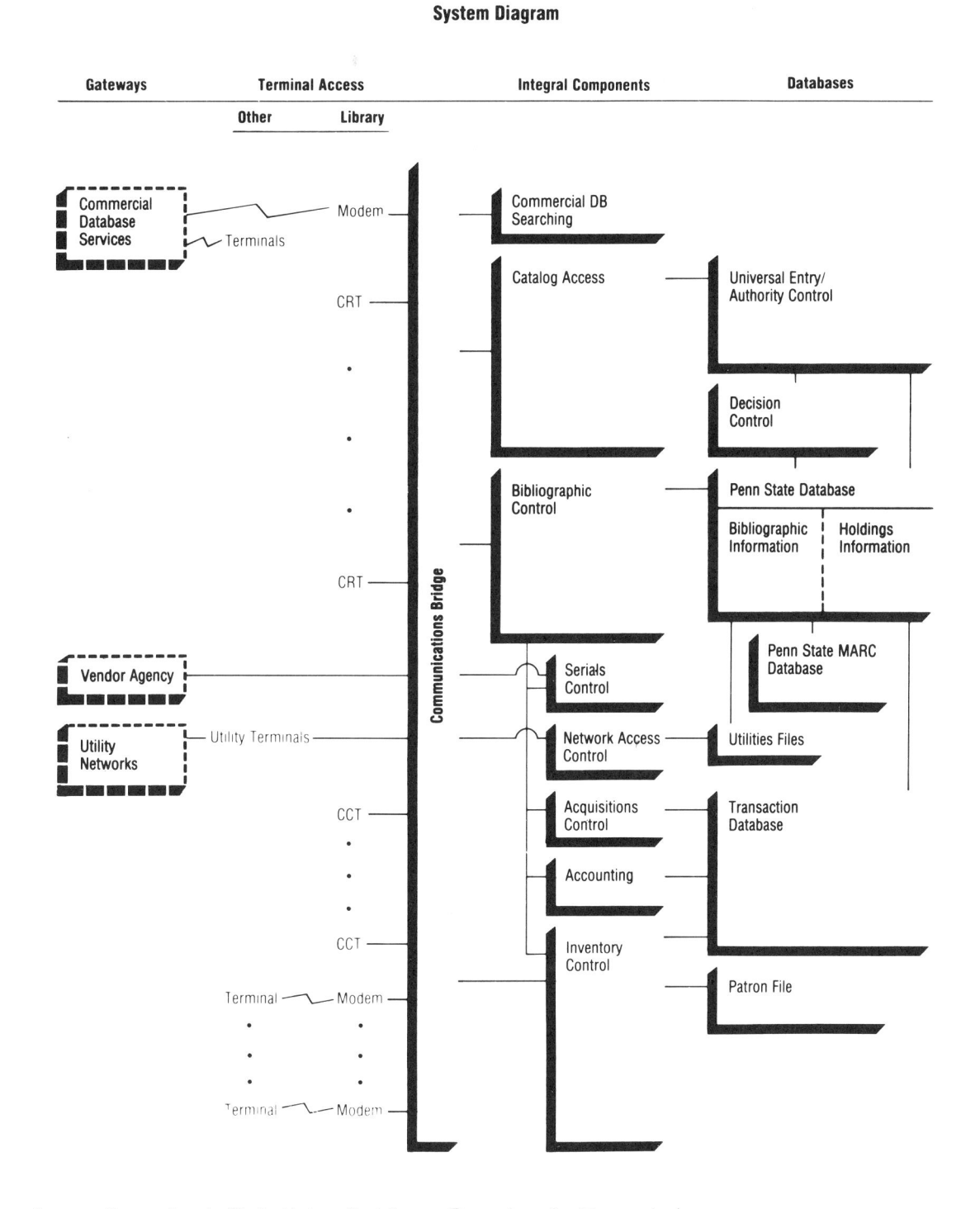

System Diagram

Source: Pennsylvania State University Library. Reproduced with permission.

Installations: Pennsylvania State University; another is being installed at the University of Tulsa.

Nature: Software-only.

Price: Prices vary according to equipment configuration. Contact vendor.

SEDNA CORPORATION (SIMS)

SIMS is a medical library-based system that was not directly derived from the ILS system. The system was developed for the University of Minnesota's Biomedical Library and configured on DEC PDP/11 equipment.

Functions and Description: Acquisitions, offline OCLC cataloging and MARC tape interfaces, fund accounting, online public access catalog and serials control. AV materials booking and circulation modules are under development. SIMS uses a specially developed operating system and offers a MARC-compatible record structure.

Equipment: Operates on DEC computers.

Installations: One academic library, one government library and two hospital libraries in stand-alone and timeshare modes. Among these are the Diehl Bio-Medical Library (University of Minnesota) and the Abbott-Northwestern Hospital Library.

Nature: Turnkey or software-only.

Price: The operating system costs $17,500 and software ranges from $24,000 to $140,000, depending on equipment configuration used.

SIRSI CORPORATION (UNICORN)

Originally developed at Georgia Tech University as a circulation system, Unicorn is now offered as an integrated system.

Functions and Description: Acquisitions, fund accounting, circulation and inventory control, and serials control which includes ordering, check-in, claiming and binding control. An online public access catalog is under development. Electronic mail is optional.

Unicorn was designed for use primarily in public and special libraries, which generally use only brief records. However, Unicorn is capable of supporting full MARC records. Tape loading and an offline interface to OCLC are available. The OCR-A type input provides a way of inputting data using spine labels or call numbers. Bar codes cannot be used. Statistics on collection use are provided through the circulation subsystem and a report generator. The system supports up to 36 terminals. The maintenance cost is generally less than most other systems.

Equipment: Operates on Zilog 8000 system with intelligent microcomputers as terminals and any computers with UNIX operating system.

Installations: Georgia Institute of Technology, Georgia Southern College, Waycross Jr. College. As of June 1984 it was being installed at Nashville State Technical Institute and a public library consortium in West Palm Beach (FL).

Nature: Turnkey.

Price: Base prices range from $20,000 to $80,000 depending on equipment configuration used, and include circulation module, installation and training. Additional software modules are available for reserves, acquisitions and serials check-in, and cost from $1000 to $5000 each. Annual software maintenance is $1000.

SWETS NORTH AMERICA, INC. (SAILS)

It is interesting to note that this British firm developed SAILS from a serials control subsystem base. Most integrated library vendors start by automating circulation or acquisitions and save the serials subsystem until last. SAILS is based on the Cullinet database management system, which is a relatively user-friendly system.

Functions and Description: Acquisitions, cataloging, circulation, fund accounting, online public access catalog and serials control. An AV materials booking module is under development and is planned for December 1984.

The serials subsystem is well developed. The menus and displays, like the system's database configuration, are comprehensive and exhaustive. SAILS has tables that automatically compute the foreign exchange rate into local dollars.

Equipment: Operates on IBM and DEC computers or on any equipment using ANSI 74 COBOL.

Installations: University of Dublin, Ireland.

Nature: Turnkey.

Price: Prices vary according to equipment configuration. Contact vendor.

SYDNEY DEVELOPMENT CORP. (EASY DATA SYSTEM)

Founded in 1978, Sydney Development Corp. is an international developer of computer business software, computer games and educational software. The original Easy Data IOLS was a special library system, developed in 1976 by Easy Data Systems of Vancouver, B.C. In 1981, a public library version was developed and Easy Data was acquired by Sydney Development Corp., which has offices in the U.S., Canada and the United Kingdom.

Functions and Description: Acquisitions, cataloging, circulation and a MARCIVE interface to produce MARC-based catalog records. Also supports word processing, accounting and electronic mail.

Equipment: Operates on Datapoint hardware and can communicate with IBM and other systems.

Installations: Public and special libraries including Everett (WA) Public Library, Chevron Research Library and Datapoint Corp. Library.

Nature: Software-only.

Price: Approximately $50,000. (Acquisitions module is $10,000, cataloging is $20,000, circulation is $15,000 and MARCIVE interface is $5000.)

UNIVERSAL LIBRARY SYSTEMS, INC. (ULISYS)

This Canadian-based firm was the fourth largest vendor of turnkey library systems in 1983 with sales in excess of $2 million. According to the vendor literature, the firm's principals have had considerable experience in computer science.

Functions and Description: Cataloging, circulation and online public access catalog. ULISYS has interlibrary loan, word processing functions and a module for producing checks for payments and vouchers. OCLC, UTLAS and WLN interfaces are available and have been selected for use by at least five libraries. Acquisitions, fund accounting and a microcomputer version capable of handling 90,000 volumes and four terminals are under development. AV materials booking and serials control modules are planned.

Essentially there are two systems; one designed to run on VAX equipment and the other on PDP. The full MARC record is retained in the VAX system but a reformatted record is kept in the PDP version. Both versions have a direct interface as well as tape interface capability. The systems management program copies data files from disk to tape each night. Portable bar code scanners are recommended for backup. The online public access catalog has two tracks; a public access and a library staff access. In addition there is a special message storage and retrieval program.

Equipment: Operates on PDP 11/23 and 24, VAX 11/750 or VAX 11/780 depending on the size of the holdings and the number of terminals.

Installations: Thirty-seven public, academic and government libraries, including Grant MacEwan Community College Library (Alberta, Canada), Clackamas County (OR) Public Library, Lake County (IN) Public Library and San Joaquin Valley Library System.

Nature: Turnkey.

Price: Base price for PDP system begins at $100,000. VAX system prices begin at $40,000 and range as high as $2 million.

VIRGINIA POLYTECHNIC INSTITUTE AND STATE UNIVERSITY (VTLS)

This system became operational in 1976 at Virginia Polytechnic Institute (VPI). It has since been installed at 34 other libraries and is being developed as a statewide, multi-type library system in West Virginia.

Functions and Description: Cataloging, circulation and online public access catalog. Word searching using Boolean operators (AND, OR, NOT), coded holdings and a comprehensive (MARC-based) authority control are other features of VTLS. Acquisitions, AV materials booking, management reports, reserve reading room control and fund accounting subsystems are planned. A serials control subsystem is under development.

The full MARC record is retained and reformatted. Data entry is possible by tape, OCLC interface or direct entry. Bar codes and OCR can be used for input. It has the ability to store, retrieve and edit serials records. Global changes to author and subject headings mean that corrections are automatically reflected in all associated bibliographic records. The ability to support multiple libraries lends the system to local or regional area networks.

VTLS can store library data in multiple databases while maintaining total data integration. Total time for loading and unloading of data is reduced by permitting sections of library data to be handled independently. It uses single, nonredundant, multi-purpose, multi-function records. Its online public access catalog functions in a non-captive environment, which allows the user to arrive or leave at any time rather than being forced to follow through a series of screens or carry on a previous user's search strategy.

In one hands-on experience, multiple hits for a given search took 20 seconds to be displayed. VTLS states that this problem (delayed search time) has been resolved with a new software technique.

Equipment: Operates on Hewlett-Packard HP 3000 Series III minicomputer with 2MB CPU and 890MB storage capacity. The MPE IV operating system is used and the programming language is COBOL.

Installations: More than 30 including academic and public libraries. The system is currently installed in Australia and New Zealand as well as various parts of the U.S. including the Youngstown State University (OH) Library and the Ohio University at Athens Library.

Nature: Turnkey or software-only.

Price: Software is $60,000 with annual maintenance of $3600. Turnkey installation for a medium-sized library with 20 terminals was approximately $200,000 in 1983. Prices vary according to equipment configuration. Contact vendor.

WARNER EDDISON ASSOCIATES, INC. (INMAGIC/BIBLIO)

Warner-Eddison Associates has provided technical library services such as cataloging, abstracting, etc. for several years. Warner has developed a database management system called INMAGIC. BIBLIO, the special library system, is one part of the broader-based database management system. BIBLIO library databases use the INMAGIC software to support the special library function.

Functions and Description: The BIBLIO application contains an online catalog, acquisitions and serials control, circulation, current awareness and information retrieval techniques for a mini- or medium-sized computer. BIBLIO provides order processing, status reports, claim notices and acquisitions lists in the ORDERS module. Serials control includes check-in, claiming, renewing and routing lists. In addition, the AWARE function provides abstract files and user profiles for current awareness.

Equipment: Operates on DEC PDP 11-RT-11, IBM System 34 or Hewlett-Packard 3000 equipment.

Nature: Software-only.

Price: $11,500 to $13,500.

WASHINGTON UNIVERSITY SCHOOL OF MEDICINE (BACS)

The Bibliographic Access and Control System (BACS) was designed and programmed by Dr. Simon Igielnik, Director of the Washington University Medical Computing Facility, in conjunction with the staff of the Access Services and Technical Services Divisions of the Washington University School of Medicine Library.

Functions and Description: Acquisitions, cataloging, circulation, online public access catalog, fund accounting and two bibliographic files (one for monographs, the other for serials). BACS' acquisitions subsystem allows ordering and receipt of items and associated fiscal control.[23] BACS has separate acquisitions and bibliographic files. The serials module is part of a nationwide serials network database for a group of 25 medical schools. All files are accessible by any terminal, restricted only by preassigned operator parameters.

When running on DEC PDP 11/40 equipment or any similar hardware configuration and using Standard MUMPS, bar code labels can be used for input. A mapping table is used to code individual MARC tags and create a more user-cordial record for the online catalog. For example, words such as author, OCLC number and title are displayed opposite each field instead of 100, 200, etc. Authority files are both machine and manually generated. Special features include word approximation searches, a spelling program and help screens.

Equipment: Operates on DEC, VAX and Plessey equipment.

Installations: Washington University Medical School and Mercer University.

Nature: Turnkey.

Price: BACS software is $20,000. MUMPS software is $10,000. Equipment to support the system costs approximately $151,000.

FOOTNOTES

1. Telephone conversation with Linda Moulton, president of BiblioTech, spring 1984.

2. Telephone conversation with representative of Bibliocentre, summer 1984.

3. Patricia Luthin, "Cataloging Marketplace," *Library Hi Tech* 1(2) (Fall 1983): 58.

4. Ibid, p. 59.

5. Dennis N. Beaumont, "The LIBS 100 System," In *Applications of Minicomputers to Library and Related Problems* (Champaign, IL: University of Illinois, Urbana-Champaign, Graduate School of Library Science, 1974), pp. 55-79.

6. *Library Systems Newsletter* 3(2) (February 1983): 12.

7. *Library Systems Newsletter* 3(11) (November 1983): 84.

8. *Library Systems Newsletter* 3(7) (July 1983): 56.

9. *Library Systems Newsletter* 3(2) (February 1983): 12.

10. John North and Elizabeth Bishop, "DOBIS/LIBIS: Online Circulation Control at Ryerson," *Library Journal* 108 (June 15, 1983): 1221-25.

11. *Advanced Technology/Libraries* (January 1980): 2.

12. *Dortmund and Leuven Library System's Librarian's Guide (Installed User Program),* SH20-2655-0. (IBM Corp., Branch Office 040, 1609 Shoal Creek Blvd., Austin, TX 78701).

13. *Library Systems Newsletter* 3(2) (February 1983): 13.

14. *Library Systems Newsletter* 3(7) (July 1983): 51-53.

15. Sandy E. Selander, et al., *The Integrated Library System (ILS) User Manual,* Lister Hill Contractor Report CR 81-06. NTIS # PB82-11496 8 (Washington, DC: National Technical Information Service, July 1981).

16. *Advanced Technology/Libraries* (December 1983): 4.

17. Richard S. Dick, "The Integrated Library System: A Historical Overview," *Information Technology and Libraries* (June 1984): 145.

18. Richard S. Dick, "The Integrated Library System," op. cit., p. 148.

19. Ibid.

20. John McGowan, "The Development of NOTIS at Northwestern," In *Conference of Integrated Online Library Systems, September 26-27, 1983: Proceedings,* rev. ed. (Canfield, OH: Genaway and Associates, 1984).

21. Patricia Luthin, "Cataloging Marketplace," op. cit.

22. *Library Systems Newsletter* 3(7) (July 1983): 49.

23. *Library Systems Newsletter* 3(11) (November 1983): 87.

7

Microcomputers and Integrated Online Library Systems

If one remembers the first huge "mainframe" computers, such as the ENIAC and UNIVAC, and considers that they were only a fraction as powerful as a modern microcomputer available in your neighborhood computer store, one realizes the enormous capabilities and future potential of microcomputers. This chapter discusses the present capabilities, limitations and applications of microcomputers as they relate to integrated online library systems. In addition, profiles are given for a number of microcomputer-based integrated systems. (Addresses and telephone numbers for the vendors listed can be found in Appendix B.)

MICROS, MINIS AND MAINFRAMES: SOME DEFINITIONS

There is considerable confusion about the definition of a "microcomputer." Even computer committees in universities seeking to establish policies on microcomputers have difficulty defining a "microcomputer" and the point at which it ceases to be a "micro" and becomes a "minicomputer."

The reason for this confusion is the rapidly changing processing and storage capacity of "microcomputers." To illustrate how dramatically computers have changed, the typical microcomputer with 64,000 characters of memory—such as a TRS-80 or an Apple—is five times more powerful than UNIVAC I, one of the first mainframe systems operating in the 1950s, with an internal storage capacity of 12,000 characters.[1]

Some use price as the criterion for distinguishing between micros and minis. They define a microcomputer as "any electronic device that processes, computes or manipulates data and costs less than $10,000." If memory is used as a criterion, then microcomputers are considered to be those with a random access (internal) memory of up to 256K, and typically 64K or 128K. Minicomputers are capable of addressing anywhere from 256K up to one megabyte or one million characters or bytes of internal memory.

112 INTEGRATED ONLINE LIBRARY SYSTEMS

If secondary storage capacity—via disk, tape or some other medium—is used to determine computer size, the present capacity of a microcomputer is about 30 megabytes (million bytes). Microcomputers with a capacity of 128K and 10 megabytes of storage are available for about $2500. Figure 7.1 shows the relationship between various computers and storage devices.

Figure 7.1: Relationships between Computers and Storage Devices

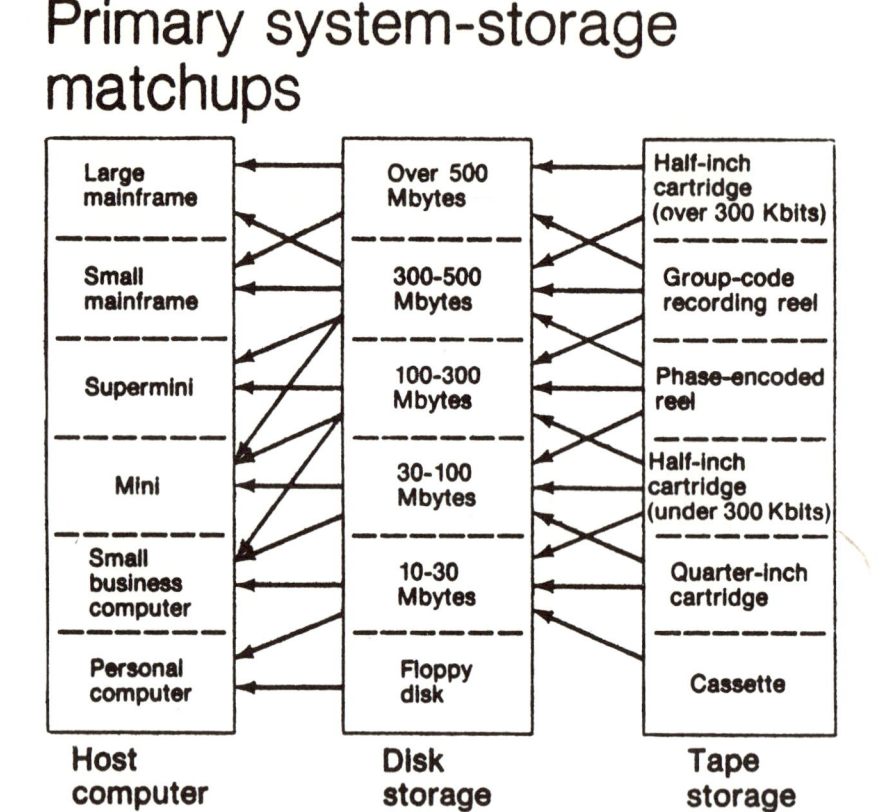

Primary system-storage matchups

Host computer	Disk storage	Tape storage
Large mainframe	Over 500 Mbytes	Half-inch cartridge (over 300 Kbits)
Small mainframe	300-500 Mbytes	Group-code recording reel
Supermini	100-300 Mbytes	Phase-encoded reel
Mini	30-100 Mbytes	Half-inch cartridge (under 300 Kbits)
Small business computer	10-30 Mbytes	Quarter-inch cartridge
Personal computer	Floppy disk	Cassette

This chart, outlining the relationships between various computers and storage devices, was compiled by Raymond C. Freeman Jr. of Freeman Associates, Santa Barbara, CA.

Source: David Weldon, "New Lift for Mass Storage: Part I. More and More Megabytes," *Computer Decisions* 15(13) (December 1983): 176. Reproduced with permission.

Currently, the terms large mainframe, small mainframe, supermini, mini, supermicro, micro, small business computer and personal computer are used to differentiate between different capabilities. The last two categories are also considered microcomputers. As the distinction between micro and minicomputers becomes more blurred, some persons have speculated that the term minicomputer will be eliminated altogether, leaving only mainframes and microcomputers. It is too early to determine whether this will happen, or whether the same terms will be retained but with changing definitions.

In this book, the term microcomputer is used for any computer that is not commonly accepted by the industry as a mainframe or minicomputer. For our purposes, a microcomputer generally costs less than $10,000, has up to 256K random access memory, can operate peripheral equipment (printers) and has at least one mass storage device (disk drive). Micros that have bubble memories, hard disk and tape drives would also be included.

A detailed discussion of microcomputers is out of the scope of this book. However, the reader is referred to other works, such as *The Librarian's Guide to Microcomputer Technology and Applications* edited by Lawrence Woods and Nolan Pope, and *Microcomputers in Libraries,* edited by Ching-Chih Chen. In addition, several periodicals report regularly on developments in microcomputer-based library systems and applications. These include *Microcomputers for Information Management: An International Journal for Library and Information Services; Online Libraries and Microcomputers; Small Computers in Libraries;* and *Library Systems Newsletter.* (Citations for these and other works are given in the bibliography at the end of this book.)

ADVANTAGES AND DISADVANTAGES OF MICROS FOR LIBRARIES

The advantages of microcomputer systems are obvious: affordability, transportability and compactness. As noted above, a microcomputer with substantial capabilities can be purchased for well under $10,000. Micros are easily installed and movable. Usually, they do not require special circuitry (although a simple spike and surge protector is advised) and they operate in a much wider variety of physical environments than mainframes. Thousands of dollars can be saved by using microcomputers that operate in an office environment instead of minicomputers requiring three- to six-ton air conditioners in separate rooms.

The chief disadvantages at present are the limited capacities for processing memory, limited mass storage space and limited number of library programs available. However, 10MB and 20MB removable cartridge disks—now available for under $4000 for most micros—have improved the storage capacity of micros greatly.

Library programs need large amounts of working memory and storage room for sorting, filing and storage of bibliographic records. The limited memory size of most micros means that large complex library programs with several subsystems and hundreds of operations cannot be readily stored in working memory. Even if such programs can fit into the memory there is no room for "scratch pads," or temporary storage space. Even if the micro can accommodate all library subsystems, it may be slow or cumbersome.

The chief drawback of most of the smaller micros is their single-task limitation. Most micros, at present, cannot perform circulation functions and acquisitions functions simultaneously or accommodate several terminals accessing a machine at the same time. Granted, even large computers only perform one task at a time, but they accomplish tasks so quickly that it at least seems simultaneous. In the case of microcomputer systems, you may have to physically remove one disk and replace it with another in order to switch from cataloging or acquisitions functions to circulation operations. Also, the speed with which tasks are accomplished is generally slower on micros than mainframes.

However, it should be noted that several manufacturers are developing micros capable of performing tasks simultaneously. Others are developing local network capabilities for microcomputers using UNIX or ZENIX operating systems. Also, new software, currently in development, will greatly accelerate processing times.

There are some microcomputer systems doing an admirable job in libraries, despite the limitations discussed above. Microcomputer library systems have been particularly useful in school and special libraries. Micros are also used as front-end processors (they perform limited tasks on data going to and from mainframes and, indeed, independently handle some tasks without going to the main CPU); interfaces (they convert the format of a record in one system to that of another system so it can be processed by the second system); emulators (they "pretend" to be terminals that a given system is looking for and can communicate with); and "smart" switching devices in communications.

MICRO-BASED IOLS

Although the majority of microcomputers are single-task oriented at this time, there are some systems that qualify as integrated library systems. As of mid-1984, these include the IOLS' offered by CL Systems Inc. (CLSI), Data Phase, DTI DataTrek, Dynix, Georgetown University Medical Center and OCLC, Inc. Brief profiles of these systems follow. (Addresses and phone numbers for the vendors listed can be found in Appendix B.) The information given is as of mid-1984. However, readers are urged to contact the vendors directly for the most up-to-date information.

CL SYSTEMS, INC. (LIBS 100 SYSTEM 23)

CL Systems' LIBS 100 System 23 has four modules available: acquisitions, circulation, online public access catalog and materials booking. The first system was installed in the Appleton (WI) Public Library in summer 1982. The system was installed in 13 libraries as of mid-1984.

The LIBS 100 System 23 operates on DEC LSI 11/23 equipment, which can accommodate touch terminals. (This system is an example of the blurring of distinctions between types of computers, as the LSI 11/23 has sometimes been referred to as a downsized minicomputer.) The system supports a 96 MB cartridge disk drive and will support up to 10 terminals or peripherals, according to company literature. The system can also be used to back up a larger system. It uses an Apple IIe as an intelligent MARC editing terminal for maintenance of the MARC record in the LIBS 100 system.

DATA PHASE SYSTEMS, INC. (EASTWIND)

Data Phase markets a micro-based IOLS called Eastwind, which runs on IBM PC or compatible equipment, Apple or Data General microcomputers. Although three modules are planned, only the circulation module is operational. The software operates as a stand-alone system. The 10 MB disk limits the total number of titles the system can handle to about 12,000 to 16,000. The cost of the software ranges from $1500 to $2500 (the price includes the acquisitions and online public access catalog modules which are under development). It can handle full or modified MARC records.

DTI DATATREK (CARD DATALOG)

Founded in 1981, DTI offers a database management system called Card Datalog. This microcomputer system features acquisitions, cataloging, serials, circulation, online public access catalog and fund accounting modules, as well as "laboratory notebooks" and communications subsystems and/or functions.

The acquisitions module checks the historical databases to determine if an item has been previously ordered and will print orders. Additional information can be included on the basic record. Once the item arrives, notices are sent to the originators of the request. Transactions and balances are generated by each "cost center." There is a deposit account report that tracks expenditures, replenishments and balances for deposit accounts. Boolean searching on any element of the database is accessible in this mode and there is integration with the other modules. Order letters, renewal notifications, an order log, monthly acquisitions reports listing title, vendor, cost, copies and publisher are generated. Figure 7.2 is a schematic representation of the Card Datalog acquisitions module.

The catalog module allows full screen editing, the creation of multiple databases and a variable number of author and subject additions. Virtually any field in the database can be searched with output to the console, printer or to a disk for further manipulation. Cards and spine labels can be printed if desirable.

The serials module can manage up to 5000 serial titles with routing slip production, global changes, overdue reports and claiming. A budget and projection report with projected percentage cost increases (useful to managers) is also available. The communications module is a bundle consisting of communications software, including a 1200 baud modem.

This is a very comprehensive and well organized IOLS that is impressive when one considers its universal adaptability to most microcomputers. Card Datalog is compatible with CP/M and MS-DOS, presently the two most standardized and prevalent operating systems in the microcomputer world. It operates on the IBM PC, Apple (with CP/M), Altos and a host of other micros using the same operating systems.

The system is oriented toward special or corporate libraries, and has an impressive list of installations. It has been installed in 31 special libraries including Apple Computer, Hughes Aircraft, McGraw Edison, Sperry Univac and First Interstate Bank.

Card Datalog is sold as software-only. Each module can be purchased independently at a cost of $2450 per module. The communications module is $495.

Figure 7.2: Card Datalog Acquisitions Module

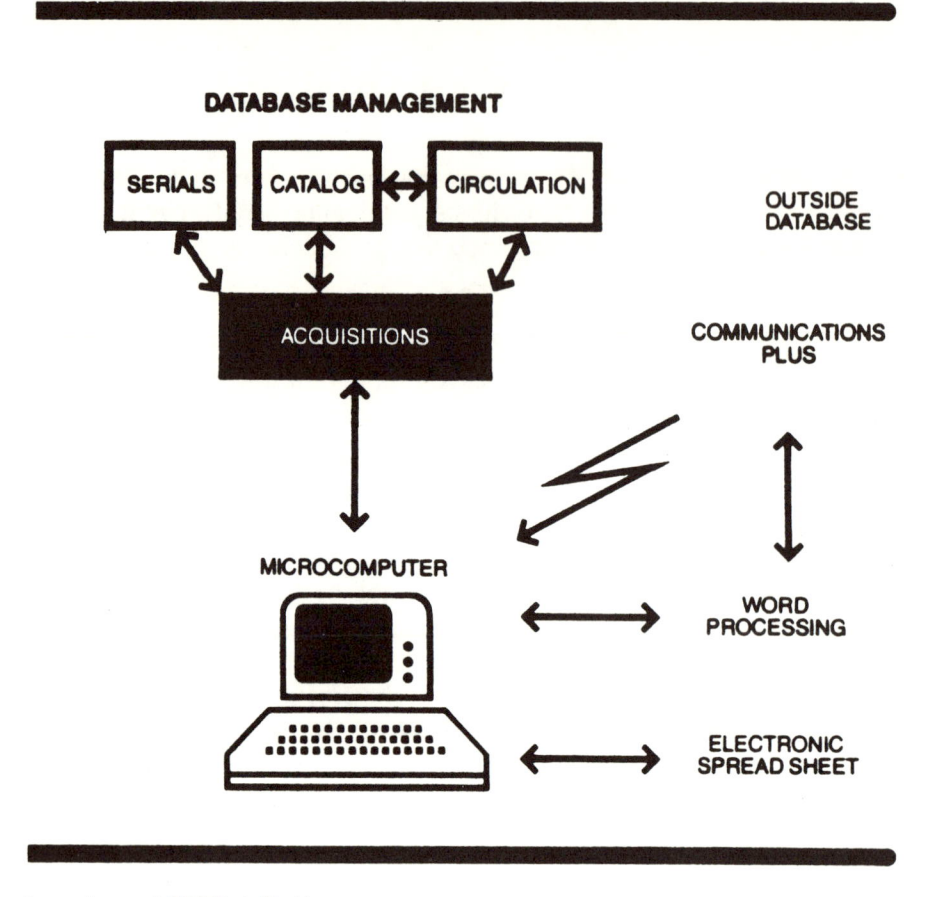

Card Datalog Acquisitions Module

(Reproduced courtesy of DTI DataTrek)

DYNIX, INC. (DYNIX)

DYNIX offers a turnkey micro-based IOLS which is aimed at the low- to medium-priced segment of the library market. Cataloging, circulation and an online public access catalog module are operational and available. Acquisitions and serials control subsystems are under development, and AV materials booking is planned.

The system operates on equipment using the PICK operating system, including Ultimate, Mentor and Datamedia computers. The first installation was in the Iberia Parish (LA) Public Library. Other installations include 10 public and four academic libraries. The system costs approximately $20,000 to $100,000 depending on the equipment configurations chosen.

GEORGETOWN UNIVERSITY MEDICAL CENTER (LIS)

Georgetown has a microcomputer version of its LIS integrated system, which supports the entire system for smaller libraries. The system runs on a Motorola Model 68 micro, with a 200 MB Winchester disk drive and a 45 MB tape backup system. The operating system is Micronetics Standard MUMPS.

OCLC, INC. (LS/2000 MICRO SERIES)

OCLC's LS/2000 Micro Series operates on DEC PDP 11/73 or 11/23 equipment with either 84 MB or 300 MB Winchester disk drives. It can support up to 10 ports or terminals and can operate in an office-type environment. Online catalog, circulation, administrative and bibliographic modules are available. The bibliographic module allows local editing and inputing with all seven MARC formats and is a stand-alone system. According to OCLC, the software is exactly the same as the larger LS/2000 system, and all operations available for the larger system are available for the micro series.

The LS/2000 Micro Series is sold as a turnkey system. The combined hardware/software costs range from $75,000 to $95,000, depending on the disk size. Maintenance is approximately $800 per month.

There are several other micro-based systems that provide most of the library functions. Although these systems usually maintain separate files, frequently not in MARC format because of limited capacity, at least one, ADLIB (offered by Advanced Library Concepts, described in Chapter 6), simulates a combined database. In this case, separate files are maintained for each module, but there is interaction between files. Hence, when a record is updated in one module, relevant records in other files are also revised (with the process being transparent to the user).

MICRO-BASED SUBSYSTEMS

Prior to the development of integrated systems that run on microcomputers, there have been a number of micro-based *subsystems* available (e.g., circulation only, acquisitions only, etc.). ComCat, CTI and Gaylord have had such subsystems operational for some time. Other microcomputer subsystems are Follett's circulation and magazine control system for Apple computers, Highsmith's Circ II for the Apple III, the MLS (Maxwell Library System) and Ringgold Management Systems' acquisitions subsystem.

In addition, several subsystems are available that act as connecting devices for messaging or reformatting records and/or processing data at the same time. There have also been several interfaces using micros, such as Innovative Interfaces' Innovacq. Various book and periodicals vendors are providing services using a microcomputer to interface between networks and to work as backups to the main system. CLSI, for example, is using the APPLE IIe both as a backup and as a training module. Microcomputers will also become increasingly used as smart modems and work stations. (More definitive coverage of the current use of micros in libraries can be found in *The Librarian's Guide to Microcomputer Technology and Applications,* by Lawrence A. Woods and Nolan F. Pope.[2]

As microcomputers become more and more powerful, it is conceivable that many of today's subsystems will become available as integrated online library systems in the not so distant future.

FUTURE OF MICRO-BASED LIBRARY SYSTEMS

Considering the rapidly changing capability of computer equipment, microcomputer-based integrated library systems will continue to develop with ever increasing capacities and will soon rival today's minicomputer systems. Total systems may evolve from single subsystems and single function microcomputer applications. In essence, the small systems will get bigger and the peripheral or single systems (such as Innovacq) are likely to expand to provide more operations and subsystems. Multiple task workstation capability will increase access to multiple databases (and possibly to other libraries in your area), and perform a wider variety of tasks in much the same way that large computer systems do today.

Finally, it should be noted that many of the criticisms leveled at micro-based library systems—for example, incompatibility and non-transferability of data among systems—apply equally to the mini and mainframe systems that exist today.

FOOTNOTES

1. Anthony Ralston, ed., *Encyclopedia of Computer Science.* (New York: Van Nostrand Reinhold Co., 1978), pp. 1440-1441.

2. Lawrence A. Woods and Nolan F. Pope, *The Librarian's Guide to Microcomputer Technology Applications.* (White Plains, NY: Knowledge Industry Publications, Inc., 1983).

Afterword:
Trends in Integrated Online Library Systems

The ideal integrated online library system would be one in which the user could sit at a CRT or keyboard, enter any search term or any part of a search term, and find virtually all references to that term, regardless of the format or database that it is in. A search would automatically be passed from the user's library, to a network, to an online database search service until "all" or "no" responses had been found. This entire process would be transparent to the user.

Acquisitions orders could build upon any information available and financial data would be automatically generated. Orders would be automatically typed and processed, and tracking of orders would be available at any access point. Holdings information would show any location (including which cart a book was on) in acquisitions, cataloging or circulation. Serials claiming would be automatic and the status of any missing or on order items would likewise be available at any point in the system. All holdings, documents, records, films, ephemeral files, etc., would be accessible and capable of being processed at any point in the system. Throughput statistics and data on use of terminals would be available instantly for management decisions.

Today, a library can get most of these features, but not necessarily with one vendor. The weakest areas of integrated systems at the present time are the linking of the library systems of diverse vendors, and connections with commercial and public databases. However, CLSI and Pennsylvania State University are beginning to provide such linkages in their systems, and other vendors are likely to follow suit. Here, we will examine some of the trends of integrated online library systems and consider some of the long-range possibilities that advances in technology may bring.

COMMUNICATION BETWEEN SYSTEMS

Interfacing different integrated online library systems so that they can communicate with each other will be a primary thrust within the near future. This will come about principally through the use of microcomputers or more powerful microprocessors. The Irving Project was one example of an attempt to achieve linkage between differing systems. The project was directed at linking automated library systems operating on diverse equipment (Data General, DEC, etc.). It was undertaken by a consortium of several Colorado libraries who sought to establish a data communications network that would allow sharing of resources through direct interactive inquiry of each participating library's public access catalog, regardless of the type of system used at each site.[1]

INCREASES IN COMPUTER CAPABILITY

Integrated databases that are truly complete will become more feasible, as storage capacities increase and cost per unit declines, allowing more bibliographic records to be added to national utility databases. This will free up more staff time to concentrate on inputting documents, audiovisual materials, microform collections and special collections. The MARC format can accommodate most types of media; hence, the vehicle for building even the most complex database is available. The largest obstacle is converting existing data to the database and creating the new records for a multi-media, multi-type record database. However, the exponential growth of storage capacity—represented by advances such as the optical digital disk and 10MB plug-in cartridges and other newer technologies—should be kept in mind by any library developing a database today.

Microcomputers will become increasingly prevalent and continue to shrink in physical size while increasing their random access memory and mass storage capacity. Programs and operating systems that heretofore have had to be composed or loaded each time the system was brought up will be stored on chips, leaving more usable memory. This will make microcomputers not only more functional as interfacing, exchanging or communication devices, but also capable of handling operating and library systems that presently require minicomputers or mainframes. Today's mainframe or minicomputer system is tomorrow's microcomputer system.

An increasing number of vendors offering single subsystems, such as acquisitions or circulation, are likely to expand into full integrated online library systems. Vendors originating in a specific type of library subsystem will increasingly move toward a more universal set of subsystems, functions and operations as they sell to other types of libraries.

Libraries, too, will experience change. Library systems will increasingly become a part of the institution's total information system. In an academic library, records will be related, and free-flowing access to student and faculty records and library records will become more prevalent for administrators and authorized personnel. For example, Washington State University has already incorporated these features in its IOLS. The impetus for this is coming from the special library world, where systems such as Datalib and BASIS are integrating the library into the total corporate information system. The concept of a total institution-wide integrated system will continue to gain momentum.

The state of the art of integrated online library systems is still in its early development, and changes within the next decade will be of tremendous magnitude. Systems installed today should have a planned replacement cycle of five to seven years, not necessarily because of deteriorating equipment, but more important, because of rapidly advancing technology in hardware and software that will make it more cost-effective to upgrade. The library administrator and his/her staff will need to maintain constant literacy with integrated online library systems. Such literacy will eventually not be an "extracurricular" luxury, but an essential part of professional survival.

FOOTNOTES

1. *Library Systems Newsletter* 3(12) (December 1983): 89-91.

Appendix A: Survey of Selected Integrated Online Library Systems

This Appendix summarizes the results of the survey of 22 vendors of integrated online library systems conducted by the author. (The survey format and methodology are explained in Chapter 5.) All data are as of April 1984. The survey is based on the information available at the time it was conducted and, hence, is not all inclusive. Also, some systems, mentioned elsewhere in this book, were too new to have an operating installation at the time of this review and therefore could not be included. The following is the key to vendor listings appearing in the Appendix.

KEY

A   ADVANCED LIBRARY CONCEPTS
B   BATTELLE SOFTWARE PRODUCTS
C   BIBLIOTECH LIBRARY SOFTWARE SYSTEMS
D   BIBLIO-TECHNIQUES LIBRARY AND INFORMATION SYSTEM
E   CALS SERVICES GROUP, LTD.
F   CARLYLE SYSTEMS, INC.
G   C.L. SYSTEMS, INC.
H   DATA RESEARCH ASSOCIATES, INC.
I   DATA PHASE SYSTEMS, INC.
J   DTI DATA TREK, INC.
K   DYNIX, INC.
L   ELECTRIC MEMORY, INC.
M   GEAC LIMITED
N   M/A-COM SIGMA DATA
O   NOTIS
P   OCLC
Q   PENNSYLVANIA STATE UNIVERSITY
R   SEDNA CORPORATION
S   SWETS NORTH AMERICA
T   UNIVERSAL LIBRARY SYSTEMS
U   VIRGINIA POLYTECHNIC INSTITUTE & STATE UNIVERSITY
V   WASHINGTON UNIVERSITY MEDICAL LIBRARY

	OA	ONA	UD	PLANNED
PART ONE: SUBSYSTEMS				
ACQUISITIONS	A B C D E G H I J M N O P R S V		K L Q T	U
AV MATERIALS BOOKING	A E G H M N	I	L R S	K P T U
CATALOGING	A B C D E G H I J K L M N O P Q R S T U V		F	
CIRCULATION	A B C E G H I J K L M N P Q S T U V	O	D F R	
FUND ACCOUNTING	A D G H I J M N O R S V	C	B Q T	E P U
ONLINE PUBLIC ACCESS CATALOG	A B C D E F G H I J K L M N O P Q R S T U V			
SERIALS CONTROL	C H J O P R S V	A B M	E K N U	D G I L T
PART TWO: SYSTEM (GENERAL)				
Online interface with bibliographic utility (OCLC, RLIN, etc.)	A D E G H I M O P Q R T V	L	B K N S	F
Ability to transfer MARC record from utility directly into in-house database.	A B D G H I M N O P Q T V		E	
Full MARC? YES NO (Circle one)	YES — A B D E F G H I L N O P Q R S T U V		NO —	
Partial MARC only? YES NO	YES —		NO — A O P	
Is FULL MARC record retained in in-house database? YES NO	YES — A B D E G H I L O P Q R S T U V		NO — K N	
Is record reformatted? YES NO	YES — A B F G K N O Q R S T U V		NO — H I P	
Can MARC records be loaded from tapes? YES NO	YES — A B D E F G H I K L N O P Q R S U V		NO —	
Various levels of access:				
View record	A B D E G H I K M N O P Q R S T V	L	F	
Edit (modify) record	A B D E G H I K M N O P Q R S T V	L	F	
Delete record	A B D E G H I K M N O P Q R S T V	L	F	
Generate management reports:				
Accounting	A D G H I J K M N O R S T		Q	V
Throughput statistics	A D E G H I K M N O P Q R S T		F	V

A Advanced Lib. Concepts
B Battelle
C Bibliotech
D Biblio-Techniques
E CALS
F Carlyle
G CLSI
H DRA
I Data Phase
J DTI
K Dynix
L EMI
M Geac
N M/A-COM
O NOTIS
P OCLC
Q Penn. State U.
R Sedna
S Swets
T Universal
U VPI
V Washington U.

	OA	ONA	UD	PLANNED
Terminal use	A D E H K M N O P Q T		F G I R	V
By search type				
Subject	H N O P Q	M	F G I	V
Author	H N O P Q	M	F G I	V
Title	H N O P Q	M	F G I	V
Backups: COM Disk Tape Printouts	G I M N O		L	
Other (specify)				
Other system-wide features (specify)				
PART THREE: SPECIFIC FUNCTIONS, OPERATIONS				
ACQUISITIONS				
Online interactive with OPAC; i.e., able to change item status on OPAC record to indicate:	E G I M N O V			
On-order	A B C D E G H I J K M N O R S		L T	
Received	A B D E G H I J K M N O R S		L T	
Bindery	A B C D E G H I K M N R S		L O T	
Display online interactive work form with prompts for original items	A B D G H I J K M N O R S V	C	T	
Generate (print) orders	B C D G H I J K M N O R S V		T	
Provision for claiming orders based on EDA	B D G H I J K M N O R S V	A	T	
Provision for processing:				
Approval plans	A B D G H I M N O R S V			
Standing orders	A B D G H I K M N O R S V			
Memberships	B D G H I J K M N O R S V	A		
Exchange agreements	B D G H I K M N O R S V	A		

A Advanced Lib. Concepts
B Battelle
C Bibliotech
D Biblio-Techniques
E CALS

F Carlyle
G CLSI
H DRA
I Data Phase
J DTI

K Dynix
L EMI
M Geac
N M/A-COM

O NOTIS
P OCLC
Q Penn. State U.
R Sedna

S Swets
T Universal
U VPI
V Washington U.

	OA	ONA	UD	PLANNED
Maintain in-process file by:				
Date	B D G H I J N O V	C R	T	
Vendor	A B D G H I J M N O S V	R	C T	
Title	A B D G H I J K M N O S V	C R	T	
Provision for donor file with addresses, amounts, etc.	B G H I N R V	M	A	
Other (specify and indicate status)				
FUND ACCOUNTING				
Ability to maintain and modify records for several accounts	A D G H I J K M N O R S V		B T	U
Maximum number of accounts/funds allowable?				
Balance or ledger sheet display of accounts	A G H I M N O R S		T	
Balance or ledger sheet display of funds	A G H I M N O R S		T	
Ability to maintain and display funds and accounts by budgeted amount	A G H I J K M N R		B	O
For each account display:				
Encumbrances (outstanding orders)	A D G H I K M N O R S V	C	B T	
Expenditures (actual payments)	A D G H I K M N O R S V	C	B T	
Free or unencumbered balance	A D G H I M N O R S V	C	B	
Ability to:				
Credit/debit accounts/funds	A D G H I J K M N O R S		B T	
Encumber/disencumber account/funds	A D G H I K M N O R S		B T	
Capability of handling prepayments	A D G H I J M N O R S V		B	

A Advanced Lib. Concepts
B Battelle
C Bibliotech
D Biblio-Techniques
E CALS
F Carlyle
G CLSI
H DRA
I Data Phase
J DTI
K Dynix
L EMI
M Geac
N M/A-COM
O NOTIS
P OCLC
Q Penn. State U.
R Sedna
S Swets
T Universal
U VPI
V Washington U.

Appendix A 127

	OA	ONA	UD	PLANNED
Provision for access to fund or accounting records by:				
Account number or category (950, 951, etc.)	ADGHIJKMNRS		CT	O
Vendor name and/or account number	AGHIJMNSV		CRT	O
Fund name (Biology department, branch, friends, etc.)	AGHIJKMNRS		CT	O
Date of issue	GHJKMS		CT	O
Invoice number	AGHIJKMRSV		T	O
Author/Title	ADGHJKMNRS		T	O
Audit trails	ADGHIKMNRS			
Can generate financial summary reports:				
Total fund activity	ADGHIKMNRSV			O
Total account activity	ADGHIJKMNRS			O
Other (specify and indicate status)				
CATALOGING				
Ability to modify any field in record	ACDEGHIJKMNOPQRSTUV	L	F	
Full screen editing	DEGHIKMNOQRSTU	L	F	
Access to records by:				
Author	ACDEGHIJKMNOPQRSTUV		F	
Title	ACDEGHIJKMNOPQRSTUV		F	
OCLC/RLIN no.	ACDGHIKMNPRSTUV		FO	
ISBN	DGHIKMNPQRSTUV		FO	
ISSN	DGHIKMNOPQRSTU		F	
Added entries	ADGHIJKMNOPQRSTUV		F	
Subject headings	ADGHIJKMNOPQRSTUV		EF	
Authority file	ABCDKNOPRSV	H	EFGI	
			MQ	

A Advanced Lib. Concepts   F Carlyle   K Dynix   O NOTIS   S Swets
B Battelle   G CLSI   L EMI   P OCLC   T Universal
C Bibliotech   H DRA   M Geac   Q Penn. State U. U VPI
D Biblio-Techniques   I Data Phase   N M/A-COM   R Sedna   V Washington U.
E CALS   J DTI

128 INTEGRATED ONLINE LIBRARY SYSTEMS

	OA	ONA	UD	PLANNED
Global find	ABCDJKLNOPRSTUV	H	EFGI MQ	
Global delete/add	ABCDJKLNOPRSUV	H	EFGI MQ	
Authority file creation while loading MARC records	ADIKNPRTUV	GHL	FM	
Workform display with prompts for original cataloging	ABDGHIJKMNOPQRSTUV		F	
Ability to indicate various locations:				
Branch libraries	ABDEGHILMNOPQTUV		F	
Multiple campuses	ABCDGHIKLMNOPQRSTU		F	
Allow for direct input of bar codes into record	ABCDEGHILMOPQRSU			
Other (specify and check status)	ADEGHIKPQSTU	BL	O	N R
CIRCULATION				
Ability to maintain inventory control over all items in library or libraries	ABCEGHIJKMNPQRSTUV	DLO	F	
Online check-in (charge)	ABCEGHIJKMNPQSTUV	LO	FR	D
Online checkout (discharge)	ABCEGHIJKMNPQSTUV	LO	FR	D
Online renewals	ABCEGHIJKMNPQSTUV	LO	FR	D
Maintain record of item activity, no. of times circulated, etc.	ACEGHIJKMPQSTU	BO	FR	
Place holds on items	ABCEGHIJKMNPQSTUV	LO	FR	
Overdues:				
Print notices	ABCEGHIJKMNPQSTUV	LO	F	
Flag patron record	ABEGHIKMPQSTUV	L	FO	J
Fines:				
Compute fines automatically	AEGHIKLMPQSTU	O	F	J
Print fine notices to patrons	AGHIKMPQSTU	LO	F	J

A Advanced Lib. Concepts
B Battelle
C Bibliotech
D Biblio-Techniques
E CALS
F Carlyle
G CLSI
H DRA
I Data Phase
J DTI
K Dynix
L EMI
M Geac
N M/A-COM
O NOTIS
P OCLC
Q Penn. State U.
R Sedna
S Swets
T Universal
U VPI
V Washington U.

Appendix A 129

	OA	ONA	UD	PLANNED
Credit or partial payment of fines	A E G H I K M P Q S T U	L	F O	J
Discharge paid fines on patron record	A E G H I K M P Q S T U	L	F O	J
Branches:				
Maintain circulation functions for branches	A B E G H I K M N P Q S T U	L O		
Maintain circulation functions for multi-campus environment	A B E G H I K M N P S T U	L O		Q
Maintain and report statistics:				
Patrons by category	A C E G H I J K M N P Q S V	L	F O	T U
Items by subject category	A C G H I J K M P Q V	B L	F O	S T U
Items by format category	A C E G H K M N P Q V	B	F O	S T U
Circle: DAILY MONTHLY ANNUALLY				
Reserve room module	A C E G I K M P Q S T V		F L O	U
Provision varying loan periods according to:				
Patron category	A C E G I K M P Q S T U V	H L O	F	
Item format or type	A E G H I K M P Q S T U V	L	F O	
Provisions for a grace period (omit fine for first five days overdue)	A E H I K M T U	L O		
Capability of changing:				
Item records	A B C E G H I J K M N P Q S T U V	L	F O	
Patron records	A B C E G H I J K M N P Q S T U V	L O	F	
Fine amounts	A E G H I K M P Q S T U	L	F O	
Input formats accepted. Indicate all.				
Bar code	A B G H I J K M P Q T U V	F O	C N	
OCR-A	A E H I P Q U	K L O	M N	
New ALS type font	S V		O	

A Advanced Lib. Concepts F Carlyle K Dynix O NOTIS S Swets
B Battelle G CLSI L EMI P OCLC T Universal
C Bibliotech H DRA M Geac Q Penn. State U. U VPI
D Biblio-Techniques I Data Phase N M/A-COM R Sedna V Washington U.
E CALS J DTI

	OA	ONA	UD	PLANNED
Cancellation of lost or stolen cards	A B E G H I J K M P Q S T U V	L O	F	
Displays:				
Books charged to patrons	A B C E G H I J K M N P Q S T U V	L	F O	
Requests by a patron	A B C E G H I J K M P Q S T U V	L	F	
Indicate item status in online public catalog:				
On shelf	A C E G H I J K M P Q S T U V	O	F L	
Checked out	A B C E G H I J K M P Q S T U V	O	F L	
On cart	A I K M P		F O	
Portable item (book) code reader for inventory and backup	A G H I M P S T		L O	
Automatic verification of patron eligibility	A B G H I K M N P Q S T U V	L O	F	
Maximum number of patron categories?				
Maximum number of material categories?				
Maximum number of subject categories?				
Record bad check-ins on patron record	A G H I K M P T	L		
Access to item records by:				
Call number	A B C E G H I K M N P Q S T U V	L O	O	
Item code	A B C E G H I J K M P Q S T U V	L	O	
Author	A B C E G H I K M P Q S T U V	L	O	
Title	A B C E G H I J K M N P Q S T U V	L		
Access to patron records by:				
Patron code number	A B C E G H I J K M N P Q S T U V	L O	F	
Name	A B C G H I J K M N P S T U V	O	F	
Social security number	A B C E H I K M P Q T U V	O	F	

A Advanced Lib. Concepts F Carlyle   K Dynix   O NOTIS   S Swets
B Battelle   G CLSI   L EMI   P OCLC   T Universal
C Bibliotech   H DRA   M Geac   Q Penn. State U.   U VPI
D Biblio-Techniques   I Data Phase   N M/A-COM   R Sedna   V Washington U.
E CALS   J DTI

Appendix A 131

	OA	ONA	UD	PLANNED
Ability to print lists of:				
Missing items	A B C E G H I K M N P Q S U V	O	F L	
Overdues	A B C E G H I J K M N P Q S T U V	L	F O	
Other (specify and indicate status)			O	
ONLINE PUBLIC CATALOG				
Ability to search records by:				
Author	A B D E F G H I J K M N O P Q R S U V	L		
Title	A B D E F G H I J K M N O P Q R S T U V	L		
Uniform title	A D E F G H I K M N O P Q R S T U	L		
Added entries	A D F G H I J K M N O P Q R S T U V	L		
Subject heading	A D F G H I J K M N O P Q R S T U V	L		
Series	A D E F G H I J K M N O P Q R S T U V	L		
By any MARC field or tag	A B E F G H I K N P		R	
Boolean searches using operators:				
AND	A B C D F G H I J K N P S V	L T	M O R U	Q
OR	A B C D F G I J N S	L T	H K M R U	P Q
NOT	A B D F G H S	T	K M O R U	P
To combine terms	A D F G H I N	T	K M O R U	P
Other (specify and indicate status)	G N O			

A Advanced Lib. Concepts	F Carlyle	K Dynix
B Battelle	G CLSI	L EMI
C Bibliotech	H DRA	M Geac
D Biblio-Techniques	I Data Phase	N M/A-COM
E CALS	J DTI	

O NOTIS	S Swets	
P OCLC	T Universal	
Q Penn. State U.	U VPI	
R Sedna	V Washington U.	

132 INTEGRATED ONLINE LIBRARY SYSTEMS

	OA	ONA	UD	PLANNED
Instring searching, i.e. will find term regardless of location in the string or field searched, title for example	A B C D E J K N P S V	H L M	O R U	G Q T
"Full text" searching. Will find term regardless of where it is located in the record	A B C F K M N P V		G O R U	Q T
Browsing by:				
Author	A B C E G H I J K M N O P Q R S U	L		F
Subject	A B C G H I J K M N O P Q S T U	L R		F
Title	A B C E G H I J K M N O P Q R S T	L		F
Call number	A C D E G H I J K M N P Q S T U V	L R	O	F
Indicate status of items displayed:				
On order	C D E G H I K M N O R S	L	Q	F P U
In-process	B C D E H I K M N O Q R S	L		F P U
Available for circulation	C E G H I J K M N P Q S T U V	L O		F
Checked-out	C E G H I K M N P Q S T U V	L O		F
On cart	I M N P T V	O		
Branch or campus location	E G H I K M N O P Q S T U V	L		
Access via acoustical coupler RS232 using phone port	B D F G H I J K M N O P Q R T U V	L		S
Displays:				
Upper/lower case	A B C D E F G H I J K M N O P Q R S T U	L		
Abbreviated record	A B C D E F G H I K M N O P Q R S T U V			
Full record	A B C D E F G H I K M N O P Q R S T U V			
Partial record	A F G H I K M P U			
Other (specify and indicate status)	M N O			

A Advanced Lib. Concepts
B Battelle
C Bibliotech
D Biblio-Techniques
E CALS

F Carlyle
G CLSI
H DRA
I Data Phase
J DTI

K Dynix
L EMI
M Geac
N M/A-COM

O NOTIS
P OCLC
Q Penn. State U.
R Sedna

S Swets
T Universal
U VPI
V Washington U.

Appendix A 133

	OA	ONA	UD	PLANNED
Statistics on terminal activity	A D E H K M O Q S T		G I L	F
No. of times used				
Type of use:				
Author	A D H O Q T	M	G I L	F
Title	A D H O Q T	M	G I L	F
Subject	A D H O Q T	M	G I L	F
Other (specify and indicate status)	O			
SERIALS				
Serials check-in	C J O R S T V	A M	E H N U	G I P Q
Serials control, claiming	C J O R S V	A I M	H N T U	G P Q
Serials routing	C R S V	A M	H N T U	G I P Q
Bindery records	C R S V	A M	H N T U	G I P Q
Other (specify and indicate status)	H O			

A Advanced Lib. Concepts F Carlyle   K Dynix   O NOTIS   S Swets
B Battelle   G CLSI   L EMI   P OCLC   T Universal
C Bibliotech   H DRA   M Geac   Q Penn. State U.   U VPI
D Biblio-Techniques   I Data Phase   N M/A-COM   R Sedna   V Washington U.
E CALS   J DTI

Appendix B: Directory of Suppliers

This Appendix is divided into four sections: vendors of total integrated online library systems; vendors of subsystems only; vendors of microcomputer systems or subsystems; and vendors of services related to IOLS (for example, data conversion). Given the dynamic nature of the library automation market, those vendors who today only offer a single subsystem (e.g., circulation) may soon develop those products into total integrated systems. Hence, they are included in this directory. (The system name appears in parentheses following the company name.)

IOLS VENDORS

Advanced Data Management (BiblioTech)
c/o Comstow Information Services
302 Boxboro Rd.
Stow, MA 01775
617-897-7163
Equipment: DEC VAX, DEC PDP 11/23 - 11/70

Advanced Library Concepts (ADLIB)
9343 Tech Center Dr.
Suite 175
Sacramento, CA 95826
916-364-0340
Equipment: IBM PC XT, Altos, Ultimate DEC, IBM 4300

Amalgamated Wireless, Ltd. (URICA)
Data Processing Systems Division
132 Arthur St.
8th Floor
North Sydney, N.S.W., 2060
Equipment: Microdata Reality 6000 or 8000, Sequel System VMS 3265, PICK operating system

Aurec Information and Directory Systems, Ltd. (ALEPH)
39 King Saul Blvd.
PO Box 33023
Tel Aviv, 61330
03-257111
Equipment: DEC VAX

Avatar Systems, Inc. (LS/2000)
11325 Seven Locks Rd.
Suite 205
Potomac, MD 20854
301-983-8900
Equipment: DEC, Data General

Battelle Software Products (BASIS)
BASIS Marketing Office
505 King Ave.
Room 11-8-112
Columbus, OH 43201
614-424-5524
Equipment: IBM, DEC, UNIVAC, CDC mainframes, DEC VAX minicomputers

Bibliocentre Division (Bibliocentre)
Centennial College
80 Cowdray Court
Scarborough, Ont M16 4N1
416-299-1516

Biblio-Techniques (BLIS)
828 E. 7th Ave.
Olympia, WA 98501
206-786-1111
Equipment: IBM 4341, Magnuson M80/42 CPU

CL Systems, Inc. (LIBS 100)
1220 Washington St.
West Newton, MA 02165
617-965-6310
Equipment: DEC 11 series, DEC VAX

CALS Services Group, Ltd. (CALS)
133 McKinstry Dr.
Elgin, IL 60120
312-697-2257
Equipment: IBM 370 or 4300 series CPU

Carlyle Systems, Inc. (TOMUS)
600 Bancroft Way
Berkeley, CA 94710
415-843-3538
Equipment: IBM, Magnuson M80132

Data Phase Systems, Inc. (ALIS)
9000 W. 67th St.
Shawnee Mission, KS 66202
913-262-5100
Equipment: Data General, Tandem

Data Research Associates, Inc. (ATLAS)
9270 Olive Blvd.
St. Louis, MO 63132
800-325-0888
Equipment: DEC, DEC VAX 780

DTI Data Trek, Inc. (DTI)
121 W. E St.
Encinitas, CA 92024
619-436-5055
Equipment: IBM PC or XT, Apple with CP/M, Altos, other CP/M-compatible systems such as Corona

Dynix, Inc. (DYNIX)
1455 W. 820 N
PO Box 714
Provo, UT 84601
801-375-2434
Equipment: Ultimate, Microdata, Prime

Electric Memory, Ltd. (EMILS/3000)
656 Munras Ave.
PO Box 1349
Monterey, CA 93942
408-646-9666
Equipment: Hewlett Packard 3000

Geac Ltd. (GLIS)
350 Steelcase Rd. W
Markham, Ontario, L3R 1B3
416-475-0525
Equipment: Geac

Georgetown University Medical Center (LIS)
Memorial Library
3900 Reservoir Rd. NW
Washington, DC 20007
202-625-7673
Equipment: DEC PDP 11/34 or 11/44 series

IBM DOBIS/LIBIS (DOBIS/LIBIS)
Library Programs Administrator
10401 Fernwood Rd.
Bethesda, MD 20817
301-897-2000
Equipment: IBM 370

Lipman Management Resources, Ltd.
(ADLIB)
54-70 Moorbridge Rd., Maidenhead
Berkshire, England, SL6 8BN
Maidenhead (0628) 37123
Equipment: Burroughs, Prime

M/A-COM Sigma Data (DATALIB)
5515 Security Lane
Rockville, MD 20852
301-984-3636
Equipment: Data General ECLIPSE, DEC VAX

Northwestern University Library (NOTIS)
1935 Sheridan Rd.
Evanston, IL 60201
312-492-7004
Equipment: IBM

NTIS (ILS)
Office of Data Base Services
5285 Port Royal Rd.
Springfield, VA 22161
703-487-4807
Equipment: Data General Eclipse, DEC PDP 11/23 to 11/70, IBM series 1

OCLC, Inc. (LS/2000)
6565 Frantz Rd.
Dublin, OH 43017
614-764-6000
Equipment: Data General
Note: OCLC acquired Avatar

Online Computer Systems, Inc. (LS/2000)
20010 Century Blvd.
Suite 101
Germantown, MD 20874
301-428-3700
Equipment: Data General

Pennsylvania State University (LIAS)
LIAS Program Office
E511 Pattee Library
University Park, PA 16802
814-865-1858
Equipment: Honeywell

Sedna Corp. (SIMS)
970 Raymond Ave.
St. Paul, MN 55114
612-647-1101
Equipment: DEC PDP 11 series

Sirsi Corp. (Unicorn)
8106 Memorial Parkway
Huntsville, AL 35802
205-881-2140
Equipment: Zilog System 8000

Swets North America, Inc. (SAILS)
PO Box 517
Berwyn, PA 19312
215-644-4944
Equipment: IBM and DEC

Sydney Development Corp. (Easy Data)
401-1200 Lonsdale Ave.
North Vancouver, B.C., V7M 3H6
604-734-8822
Equipment: Datapoint

Universal Library Systems (ULISYS)
205-1571 Bellevue Ave.
West Vancouver, B.C., V7V 1A6
604-926-7421
Equipment: DEC, VAX 11/780

Virginia Polytechnic Institute and State University (VTLS)
Virginia Tech Library Automation Project
416 Newman Library
Blacksburg, VA 24061
703-961-5847
Equipment: Hewlett Packard 3000

Warner-Eddison Associates, Inc.
(INMAGIC)
186 Alewife Brook Parkway

Cambridge, MA 02138
617-661-8124
Equipment: DEC, Hewlett Packard, IBM System 34

Washington University School of Medicine (BACS)
Medical Library
4580 Scott Ave.
St. Louis, MO 63110
314-454-3711
Equipment: DEC PDP 11

SUBSYSTEM VENDORS

Blackwell Library Systems, Inc. (PERLINE/BOOKLINE)
310 E. Shore Rd.
Room 204
Great Neck, NY 11023
516-466-5418
Subsystems: Serials
Equipment: DEC or Plessy

Brodart, Inc. (OLAS)
1609 Memorial Ave.
Williamsport, PA 17705
800-233-8467
Subsystems: Acquisitions
Equipment: Any asynchronous terminal

CLASS (Checkmate, Golden Retriever)
1415 Koll Circle
Suite 101
San Jose, CA 95112
408-289-1756
Subsystems: Serials control, provides access to RLIN by subject, etc.
Equipment: TRS-80

Colorado Computer Systems, Inc. (COMCAT)
3005 W. 74th Ave.
Westminster, CO 80030
303-426-5880
Subsystems: OPAC on a microcomputer
Equipment: Apple IIe

Cuadra Associates, Inc. (STAR)
1523 6th St.
Suite 12
Santa Monica, CA 90401
213-451-0644
Subsystems: Catalog and interface
Equipment: Alpha Micro

Ebsco Industries, Inc. (Ebsconet)
PO Box 1943
Birmingham, AL 35282
205-991-6600
Subsystems: Serials
Equipment: Anderson Jacobson 510 and 520, Hazeltine, DEC

F. W. Faxon Co., Inc. (LINX)
15 S.W. Park
Westwood, MA 02090
800-225-6055
Subsystems: Serials
Equipment: Numerous systems. Contact vendor.

Follett Book Company (Book Trak)
4506 N.W. Highway
Crystal Lake, IL 60014
800-435-6170
Subsystems: Cataloging, circulation, serials control
Equipment: Apple II+

Gaylord Brothers, Inc. (GS series 100, 600, 2000)
PO Box 4901
Syracuse, NY 13221
800-448-6160
Subsystems: Acquisitions, circulation, catalog, serials control
Equipment: Apple IIe, Datapoint 8200

Highsmith Co. (Circa I, Circa II)
PO Box 800
Fort Atkinson, WI 53538
800-558-2110
Subsystems: Circulation
Equipment: Apple IIe, IBM/PC-XT

Innovative Interfaces, Inc. (INNOVACQ)
2131 University Ave. #334
Berkeley, CA 94704
415-540-0880
Subsystems: Acquisitions, interface
Equipment: Custom

Maxwell Library Systems (MLS)
186 Alewife Brook Parkway
Cambridge, MA 02138
617-623-2323
Subsystems: Circulation
Equipment: Apple IIe

MetaMicro Library Systems, Inc.
311 W. Laurel
Suite 211
San Antonio, TX 78212
512-224-8455
Subsystems: Serials control, cataloging

Equipment: Southwest Technical Products (SWTP)

R. R. Bowker (BAS)
205 E. 42nd St.
New York, NY 10017
212-916-1727
Subsystems: Book acquisition
Equipment: Any terminal with communications capability

Ringgold Management Systems, Inc. (Nonesuch)
PO Box 368
Beaverton, OR 97075
503-645-3502
Subsystems: Acquisitions
Equipment: Microcomputers using COBOL language

TPS Electronics
4047 Transport
Palo Alto, CA 94303
415-856-6833
Subsystems: Interface, bar code readers
Equipment: Apple II

Uniface (BITS)
Midwest Library Service
11443 St. Charles Rock Rd.
Bridgeton, MO 63044
800-325-8833
Subsystems: Acquisitions, catalog card production, interface
Equipment: IBM PC

MICROCOMPUTER LIBRARY SUBSYSTEMS

Advanced Library Concepts (ADLIB)
9343 Tech Center Dr.
Suite 175
916-364-0340
Subsystems: Acquisitions, cataloging, circulation
Equipment: Altos, IBM PC XT, IBM 4300, Ultimate DEC

CL Systems, Inc. (LIBS 100)
1220 Washington St.
West Newton, MA 02165
617-965-6310
Subsystems: Acquisitions, AV materials booking, Boolean search, cataloging, circulation, fund accounting, OPAC
Equipment: DEC 11 series, DEC VAX

CLASS (Checkmate, Golden Retriever)
1415 Koll Circle
Suite 101
San Jose, CA 95112
408-289-1756
Subsystems: Serials control, access to RLIN by subject, etc.
Equipment: TRS-80

Colorado Computer Systems, Inc. (COMCAT)
3005 W. 74th Ave.
Westminster, CO 80030
303-426-5880
Subsystems: OPAC
Equipment: Apple IIe

Data Phase Systems, Inc. (Eastwind)
9000 W. 67th St.
Shawnee Mission, KS 66202
913-262-5100
Subsystems: Acquisitions, cataloging, circulation, fund accounting, OPAC
Equipment: Data General, Tandem

DTI Data Trek, Inc. (Card Datalog)
121 W. E St.
Encinitas, CA 92024
619-436-5055
Subsystems: Acquisitions, cataloging, circulation, serials
Equipment: IBM PC or XT, Apple with CP/M, Altos, other CP/M compatible systems

Dynix, Inc. (Dynix)
1455 W. 820 N
PO Box 714
Provo, UT 84601
801-375-2434
Subsystems: Circulation, OPAC
Equipment: Ultimate, Mentor, Datamedia

Follett Book Company (Book Trak)
4506 N.W. Highway
Crystal Lake, IL 60014
800-435-6170
Subsystems: Cataloging, circulation, serials control
Equipment: Apple II+

Gaylord Brothers, Inc. (GS series 100, 600, 2000)
PO Box 4901
Syracuse, NY 13221
800-448-6160
Subsystems: Acquisitions, circulation, catalog, serials control
Equipment: Apple IIe, Datapoint 8200

Highsmith Co. (Circa I, Circa II)
PO Box 800
Fort Atkinson, WI 53538
800-558-2110
Subsystems: Circulation
Equipment: Apple IIe, IBM/PC-XT

OCLC, Inc. (LS/2000 System 23)
6565 Frantz Rd.
Dublin, OH 43017
614-764-6000
Subsystems: Cataloging, circulation, OPAC
Equipment: Data General

TPS Electronics
4047 Transport
Palo Alto, CA 94303
415-856-6833
Subsystems: Interface, bar code readers
Equipment: Apple II

UNIFACE (BITS)
Midwest Library Service
11443 St. Charles Rock Rd.
Bridgeton, MO 63044
800-325-8833
Subsystems: Acquisitions, catalog card production, interface
Equipment: IBM PC

VENDORS OF IOLS-RELATED SERVICES

Auto-Graphics
751 Monterey Pass Rd.
Monterey Park, CA 91754
213-269-9451
Service: Retrospective conversion

Carrollton Press, Inc.
1911 Fort Meyer Dr.
Arlington, VA 22209
800-368-3008
Service: Retrospective conversion

CLASS
1415 Koll Circle
Suite 101
San Jose, CA 95112
408-289-1756
Service: Online subject access to RLIN, microbased serials control

Cuadra Associates, Inc.
1523 6th St.
Suite 12
Santa Monica, CA 90401
213-451-0644
Service: Interface, reformatting data

Easy Data Systems, Ltd.
401-1200 Lonsdale Ave.
North Vancouver, B.C., V7M 3H6
604-734-8822
Service: Processes MARC based catalog records

General Research Corp.
Library Systems
PO Box 6770
Santa Barbara, CA 93160-6770
800-235-6788
Service: Retrospective conversion, COM catalogs

James E. Rush Associates, Inc.
2223 Carriage Rd.
Powell, OH 43065-9703
614-881-5949
Service: Library Systems evaluation guides

Selected Bibliography

"Acquisitions/Circulation Interface." Special issue. *Library and Acquisitions: Practice and Theory* 4 (1980).

Advanced Technology/Libraries (AT/L). Published monthly by Knowledge Industry Publications Inc., 701 Westchester Ave., White Plains, NY 10604.

Auerbach Computer Technology Reports. Several series: *Computer Systems; Business Minicomputer Systems; General Purpose Mini-Computers; Plug Compatible Peripherals; Standard Peripherals,* et al. Auerbach Publishers, Inc., 6560 N. Park Dr., Pennsauken, NJ 08109.

Bahr, Alice Harrison. *Automated Library Circulation Systems, 1979-80.* 2nd ed. White Plains, NY: Knowledge Industry Publications, Inc., 1979.

Baker, Betsy, and Neilsen, Brian. "Educating the Online Catalog User: Experiences and Plans at Northwestern University Library." *Research Strategies* 1 (Fall 1983): 155-166.

Beaumont, Dennis N. "The LIBS 100 System." In *Applications of Minicomputers to Library and Related Problems: Proceedings of the 1974 Clinic on Library Applications of Data Processing.* Urbana, IL: University of Illinois Graduate School of Library Science, 1974.

Boss, Richard W. *Automating Library Acquisitions: Issues and Outlook.* White Plains, NY: Knowledge Industry Publications, Inc., 1982.

Boss, Richard W. *The Library Manager's Guide to Automation.* 2nd ed. White Plains, NY: Knowledge Industry Publications, Inc., 1984.

Boss, Richard W., and McQueen, Judy. "Automated Circulation Control Systems." *Library Technology Reports* 18 (March/April 1981): 125-237.

Burch, John G., Jr.; Strater, Felix R.; and Grudnitski, Gary. *Information Systems: Theory and Practice*. 2nd ed. New York: John Wiley & Sons, 1979.

Carter, Ruth C., and Bruntjen, Scott. *Data Conversion*. White Plains, NY: Knowledge Industry Publications, Inc., 1983.

Chapman, Edward A.; St. Pierre, Paul L.; and Lubans, John, Jr. *Library Systems Analysis Guidelines*. New York: Wiley-Interscience, John Wiley & Sons, 1970.

Chen, Ching-Chih, and Bressler, Stacey E., eds. *Microcomputers in Libraries*. New York: Neal-Schuman Publishers, Inc., 1982.

Corey, James F.; Spalding, Helen L.; and Fraser, Jeanmarie Lang. "Involving Faculty and Students in the Selection of a Catalog Alternative." *The Journal of Academic Librarianship* 8 (January 1983): 328-333.

COSMIC: A Catalog of Selected Computer Programs. Published by the National Aeronautics and Space Administration. Available from the Computer Center Management and Information Center (COSMIC), 112 Barrow Hall, University of Georgia, Athens 30602.

Datapro Reports. Several series: *Datapro 70: The EDP Buyers Bible; Minicomputers; Communications, Directory of Small Computers,* et al. Datapro Research Corporation, 1805 Underwood Blvd., Delran, NY 08075.

DeGennaro, Richard. "Library Automation and Networking Perspectives on Three Decades." *Library Journal* 108 (April 1, 1983): 629-635.

DeGennaro, Richard. "Library Automation: Changing Patterns and New Directions." *Library Journal* 101 (January 1976): 175-183.

Dortmund and Leuven Library Systems Librarian's Guide (Installed User Program). SH20-2655-0. IBM Corp., Branch Office 040, 1609 Shoal Creek Blvd., Austin, TX 78701. (1982).

Dortmund and Leuven Library Systems under SSX/VSE. Program No. 5785-DLP SB11-5868-0, File number S370/4300-64. IBM Netherlands, International Field Proghram Center, P.O. Box 24, 1420 A UITHOORN, Netherlands. (1983).

Epstein, Susan Baerg. "Buy, Build Adapt—or Forget It!" *Library Journal* 108 (May 1, 1983): 888-889.

Fayen, Emily Gallup. *The Online Catalog: Improving Public Access to Library Materials*. White Plains, NY: Knowledge Industry Publications, Inc., 1983.

Freedman, Maurice J. "Library Automation: Five Case Studies." *LJ Special Report* 22 (1982).

Genaway, David C. "The Five Cs of Automation: Computers, Contracts, Cooperation, Concessions, Conviviality." *Technicalities* 2 (April 1981): 11-12.

Genaway, David C. "Microcomputers as Interfaces to Bibliographic Utilities." *Online* 7 (May 1983): 21-27.

Genaway, David C., ed. and comp. *Conference on Integrated Online Library Systems, September 26-27, 1983; Proceedings,* rev. ed. Canfield, OH: Genaway & Associates, Inc. 1984.

Goldstein, Charles M.; Payne, Elizabeth A.; and Dick, Richard S. "Integrated Library System (ILS): System Overview." NTIS report no. PB81-188039.

Goldstein, Charles M., and Richard S. Dick. "The Lister Hill Center Integrated Library System (ILS)." *National Library of Medicine News* 35 (1) (January 1980): 1-2.

Grosch, Audrey N. *Minicomputers in Libraries, 1981-82: The Era of Distributed Systems.* White Plains, NY: Knowledge Industry Publications, Inc., 1982.

Hildreth, Charles R. *Online Public Access Catalogs: The User Interface.* Dublin, OH: OCLC, 1982.

Horny, Karen L. "NOTIS-3 (Northwestern On-line Total Integrated System): Technical Services Applications." *Library Resources & Technical Services* 22 (Fall 1978): 361-367.

Horny, Karen L. "Online Catalogs: Coping with the Choices." *The Journal of Academic Librarianship* 8 (March 1982): 14-19.

"Integrated Library Information Systems in ARL Libraries." Special Kit 90. Washington, DC: Association of Research Libraries, Office of Management Studies, Systems Procedures Exchange Center, 1983.

Lawrence, Gary S.; Matthews, Joseph R.; and Miller, Charles E. "Costs and Features of Online Catalogs: The State of the Art." *Information Technology and Libraries* 2 (December 1983): 409-449.

Library Hi Tech (Published quarterly) and *Library Hi Tech News* (published eleven times per year). Published by Pierian Press, P.O. Box 1808, Ann Arbor, MI 48106.

Library Hotline. Published weekly (except July and August) by R.R. Bowker Co., 205 E. 42nd St., NY, NY 10017.

Library Systems Evaluation Guides. 8 volumes. James E. Rush Associates, Inc., 2223 Carriage Rd., Powell, OH 43065-9703.

Library Systems Newsletter. Published monthly by Library Technology Reports, American Library Association, 50 E. Huron St., Chicago, IL 60611.

Library Technology Reports. Published bimonthly by the American Library Association, 50 E. Huron St., Chicago, IL 60611.

Lisowski, Andrew, and Sessions, Judith. "Selecting a Retrospective Conversion Vendor." *Library Hi Tech* 1 (Spring 1984): 65-68.

Luthin, Patricia. "Cataloging Marketplace." *Library Hi Tech* 1 (Fall 1983): 53-62.

Matthews, Joseph R. "Competition & Change: The 1983 Automated Library System Marketplace." *Library Journal* 109 (May 1, 1984): 853-860.

Matthews, Joseph R. *Public Access to Online Catalogs: A Planning Guide for Managers.* Weston, CT: Online, Inc., 1982.

Matthews, Joseph R.; Lawrence, Gary S.; and Ferguson, Douglas K. *Using Online Catalogs: A Nationwide Survey.* New York: Neal-Schuman Publishers, Inc. 1983.

Microcomputers for Information Management: An International Journal for Library and Information Services. Published quarterly by Ablex Publishing Corp., 355 Chestnut St., Norwood, NJ 07648.

Microcomputers for Libraries. Published quarterly by James E. Rush Associates, Inc., 2223 Carriage Rd., Powell, OH 43065-9703.

North, John, and Bishop, Elizabeth. "DOBIS/LIBIS: Online Circulation Control at Ryerson." *Library Journal* 108 (June 15, 1983): 1221-1225.

Nyren, Karl and Berry, John. "Information & Technology: at the Crossroads." *Library Journal* 108 (November 1, 1983): 2017-2022.

Online Libraries and Microcomputers. Published monthly by Information Intelligence, P.O. Box 31098, Phoenix, AZ 85046.

Online: the Magazine of Information Systems. Published six times a year by Online, Inc., 11 Tannery Lane, Weston, CT 06883.

Post, William E., and Watson, Peter C., eds. *Online Catalog: The Inside Story: A Planning & Implementation Guide.* Chico, CA: Ryan Research International, 1983.

Richards, Timothy. "The Online Catalog: Issues in Planning and Development." *The Journal of Academic Librarianship* 10 (March 1984): 4-9.

Sager, Donald J. *Public Library Administrators' Planning Guide to Automation.* Dublin, OH: OCLC, 1983.

Selander, Sandy E.; Payne, Elizabeth A.; Freiburger, Gary; and Brogan, Linda B. *The Integrated Library System (ILS): User Manual.* Lister Hill Contractor Report CR 81-06. NTIS PB82-11496 8. Springfield, VA: National Technical Information Service, 1981.

Small Computers in Libraries. Published monthly (except July and August) by SCIL, Graduate Library School, College of Education, University of Arizona, 1515 E. First St., Tucson, AZ 85719.

"Special Section: ILS and LS/2000." *Information Technology & Libraries* 3 (June 1984): 144-173, 209-214.

Technicalities. Published monthly by Oryx Press, 2214 N. Central, Encanto, Phoenix, AZ 85004.

Tolle, John E. *Public Access Terminals: Determining Quantity Requirements.* Dublin, OH: OCLC, 1984.

Woods, Lawrence A., and Pope, Nolan F. *The Librarian's Guide to Microcomputer Technology and Applications.* White Plains, NY: Knowledge Industry Publications, Inc., 1983.

Index

Abbott-Northwestern Hospital Library, 104
ADLIB. *See* Advanced Library Concepts and Lipman Management Resources, Ltd.
Advanced Data Management, 82-83
Advanced Library Concepts, 83
AG Database Machine, 86
Air Force Library (Maxwell Air Force Base), 99
ALEPH. *See* Aurec Information & Directory Systems, Ltd.
ALIS. *See* Data Phase Systems, Inc.
Altos, 83
Amalgamated Wireless, Ltd., 83
Amherst College, 100
Apple Computer, Inc., 111, 114-115, 117
Army Library, 98
Association of Research Libraries, 4
ATLAS. *See* Data Research Associates, Inc.
Auerbach Pubs., Inc., 32, 40
Aurec Information & Directory Systems, Ltd., 83-84
Autographics, Inc., 38, 59
Avatar Systems, Inc., 37, 68, 84, 98, 100-101
  See also OCLC

BACS. *See* Washington University Medical School
Baltimore County Public Library, 89
Barkalow, Pat, 4, 19
BASIS. *See* Battelle
Battelle, 17, 84-85
Bibliocentre. *See* Bibliocentre Division, Centennial College
Bibliocentre Division, Centennial College, 85-86
Biblioteca National, 100
Bibliotech. *See* Advanced Data Management
Biblio-Techniques, Inc., 86

Biblio-Techniques Library and Information System, 46; 86
Blair, John, 41
Books in Print, 5
BRS, 3, 17, 102

CALS. *See* CALS Service Group, Ltd.
CALS Services Group, Ltd., 87
Card Datalog. *See* DTI DataTrek
Carlyle Systems, Inc., 69, 87
Carnegie Mellon, 101
Carnegie-Stout (IA) Public Library, 89
Carrollton Press, Inc., 59
Carter, Ruth C., 59
Chabot College (CA), 91
Chapman, Edward, 1, 7
Chen, Ching-Chih, 113
Chevron Research Library, 106
CL Systems, Inc. (CLSI), 7, 36, 46, 51, 68, 70, 88-89, 114
Clackamas County (OR) Public Library, 106
Claremont College, 7, 100
Cleveland Public Library, 88, 91
College of DuPage Learning Resource Center, 89
Columbia University, 86
Comcat, 117
Computerworld, 32
Comstow Information Services. *See* Advanced Data Management
Connecticut Consortium Libraries On Line, 89
Contracts, 52-54
Control Data Corp. (CDC), 85, 89, 92
Coyle, Mary, 17-18
CTI Library Systems, Inc., 117
Cullinet, 105

Dallas County Community College, 89

147

Data Conversion, 59
Data conversion, 38-39, 58-59
Data General Corp., 90, 97, 99-102, 114
DATALIB. *See* M/A-COM Sigma Data, Inc.
Data Link, 88
Datamedia Corp., 116
Data Phase Systems, Inc., 46, 67-69, 89-90, 114-115
Datapoint Corp., 106
Datapro Research Corp., 32, 40
Data Research Associates, Inc. (DRA), 37, 68-70, 90-91
  Library for the Blind, 7
De Gennaro, Richard, 2, 65
Dialog Information Services, Inc., 3, 88, 102
Dick, Richard S., 100
Digital Equipment Corp. (DEC), 82-85, 89, 91, 95, 97, 99, 101-102, 104-105, 108-109, 114
Dortmund Library System, 94
DRS, 82
DTI DataTrek Inc., 114-116
Dynix Inc., 114, 116

East Carolina University, 99
Eastwind. *See* Data Phase Systems, Inc.
Easy Data System. *See* Sydney Development Corp.
Electric Memory, Inc., 91-92
Elgin Community College, 87
EMILS/3000. *See* Electric Memory, Inc.
ENIAC, 111
Epstein, Susan Baerg, 51, 57
Evanston/Chicago Campus Library, 100
Everett (WA) Public Library, 106

F.W. Faxon Co., Inc., 92, 102
First Interstate Bank, 115

Gaylord Bros., Inc., 117
Geac Ltd., 21, 46, 68, 70, 92-93
Georgetown University School of Medicine, 6, 93, 114, 117
Georgia Institute of Technology, 105
Georgia Southern College, 105
Georgia Tech University, 104
German, R.A., 92
GLIS. *See* Geac Ltd.
GM Tech Center Library, 97
Grant MacEwan Community College Library, 106

Hampshire College, 100
Harvard University, 2
Hazeltine, 44
Hebrew University, 83
Hewlett-Packard Co., 91, 107-108
Honeywell Information Systems, Inc., 83, 102
Hughes Aircraft, 115

Iberia Parish (LA) Public Library, 116
IBM Corp., 6-7, 46, 83, 85-88, 94-96, 100, 105-106, 108, 114
Igielnik, Dr. Simon, 108
Illinois Valley Community College of Oglesby, 87
ILS. *See* National Library of Medicine
INMAGIC/BIBLIO. *See* Warner Eddison Associates, Inc.
Installed User Program: Librarian's Guide, 95
Integrated online library system (IOLS)
  comparing costs, 39-40
  defined, 4-5
  development of, 6-7
  environment for, 54-56
  hardware for, 45
  overview of, 5-6
  planning for, 15-21
  principles of operation, 7-9
  profiles of, 81-110
  selecting and evaluating systems, 31, 33, 42, 60, 65
  software for, 45
  subsystems, 68-70, 117-118
Isserstedt, R.K., 92

Johns Hopkins University, 86

Kennedy, 92

Lear Seigler, 44, 89
Leuven Library System, 94
LIAS. *See* Pennsylvania State University
Librarian's Guide to Microcomputer Technology and Applications, 113
Library and Information Technology Association (LITA), 4, 38
Library automation, 1-4
Library Journal, 34
Library Literature, 4
Library of Congress, 2, 46
Library Systems Newsletter, 18, 113

Index 149

LIBS 100. *See* CL Systems, Inc.
Lipman Management Resources, Ltd., 96
LIS. *See* Georgetown University School of Medicine
Lister Hill National Center for Biomedical Communications, 6, 97
    See also National Library of Medicine (NLM)
LMR Information Systems, 10
Logan (UT) Public Library, 91
LS/2000. *See* OCLC, Inc.

McAllister, Caryl and Stratton, 94
McGraw Edison, 115
M/A-COM Sigma Data, Inc., 68-70, 96-97
Magnuson, 86, 88
Mainframe, 111-113
Marin County (CA) Public Library, 88
Maxwell Library System, 117
MELVYN, 86
Memphis State University Library, 89
Mentor Computers, 116
Mercer University, 109
Microcomputer
    advantages and disadvantages of, 113-114
    defined, 111-113
Microcomputers for Information Management: An International Journal for Library and Information Services, 113
Microcomputers in Libraries, 113
Microdata Reality, 83
Minicomputer, 111-113
MITRE Corp., 17
Motorola, Inc., 94-117
Mount Holyoke College, 101

Nashville State Technical Institute, 105
National Library of Canada, 85
National Library of Medicine (NLM), 4, 7, 11, 37, 93
    Integrated Library System (ILS), 97-101
    See also Lister Hill Center for Biomedical Communications
National Technical Information Service (NTIS), 98-99
National Union Catalog, 2
New York Public Library Research Library, 2, 88
New York University, Bobst Library, 58
Nook, Cathryn, 59

Northeastern Ohio Universities College of Medicine, 41
Northwestern University, 2, 6, 11, 68, 99-100
Norton, Nancy, 59
NOTIS, 46, 67-69
    See also Northwestern University

OCLC, Inc., 2, 7, 29, 43, 58-59, 68, 82, 84, 87, 89, 92, 97-102, 104-107, 114, 117
Ohio University at Athens Library, 107
Ohio Wesleyan University, 100
Online Computer Systems, Inc., 98, 100-102
    See also OCLC, Inc.
Online Libraries and Microcomputers, 113

Pasadena Public Library, 19
Pennsylvania State University, 102-104
Pentagon Library, 98
Persky, Gail, 58
Plessey, 95, 109
Pope, Nolan, 113
Prime Computer, Inc., 83, 96
Providence (RI) Public Library, 89

Research Libraries Information Network (RLIN), 58-59, 68, 89, 92, 102
Ringgold Management Systems, 117
Ryerson Polytechnic, 95

SAILS. *See* Swets North America, Inc.
St. Pierre, Paul, 1, 7
San Francisco Public Library, 88
San Joaquin Valley Library System, 106
Schlumberger Doll Research Library, 97
SDC Information Services, 3
Sedna Corp., 104
Sequel System, 83
SIMS. *See* Sedna Corp.
Sirsi Corp., 104-105
Small Computers in Libraries, 113
Smith College, 101
Smithsonian Library, 92
Sperry Univac, 115
Stanford University, 2, 6
Stroum, Richard, 51
Swets North America, Inc., 105
Sydney Development Corp., 105-106

Tandem Computers, Inc., 90
TOMUS. *See* Carlyle Systems, Inc.

TRS-80, 111

ULISYS, 46
   See also Universal Library Systems, Inc.
Ultimate, 116
Unicorn. *See* Sirsi Corp.
UNIVAC, 85, 111
Universal Library Systems, Inc., 42, 52, 106
University of Akron, 100
University of California at San Diego, 86
University of Chicago, 2, 6, 11
University of Cincinnati Libraries, 34
University of Dortmund, 94
University of Dublin, 105
University of Hawaii at Manoa, 83
University of Leuven, 85, 94
University of Massachusetts, 101
University of Minnesota Diehl Bio-medical Library, 6, 104
University of Missouri, 31
University of Newcastle, 101
University of Texas Health Science Center at San Antonio, 94
University of Toronto, 2

University of Tulsa, 104
URICA. *See* Amalgamated Wireless, Ltd.
UTLAS, 43, 89, 92

Virginia Polytechnic Institute and State University, 107-108
Virginia Tech Library System, 21, 45-46, 69, 107
   See also Virginia Polytechnic Institute and State University

Wang Laboratories, Inc., 85
Warner Eddison Associates, Inc., 108
Washington Library Network (WLN), 6, 43, 59, 86, 89
Washington University Medical School, 6, 108-109
Waycross Jr. College, 105
Woods, Lawrence, 113

Youngstown State University, 24, 34, 107

Zilog, Inc., 105

ABOUT THE AUTHOR

David C. Genaway is the University Librarian (administrator) of the William F. Maag Library at Youngstown State University (Youngstown, OH), where he was responsible for the selection and implementation of an integrated online library system, and is secretary for the university's Computer Advisory Committee. He is president of Genaway & Associates, Inc., an information/research management consulting firm, and sponsor of the national Conferences on Integrated Online Library Systems. He has been involved with library and information science for nearly two decades, primarily in the areas of administration, automation, organization and development.

Previously, Dr. Genaway was responsible for the reclassification and automation of the shelf list at Central Washington State University, the development of Senator Karl E. Mundt's archival library and has taught technical processes and audiovisual library media courses at the Peabody Library School of Vanderbilt University. He has been a consultant to the Country Music Hall of Fame Library, Winrock International, and other organizations.

Dr. Genaway was editor and compiler of the *Conference on Integrated Online Library Systems, September 26-27, 1983: Proceedings.* His articles on library science and automation have appeared in *Online Library Journal, Technicalities* and other publications. He holds a Ph.D. from the University of Minnesota, and an M.L.S. from the University of Michigan.

©OPYRIGHT

Guide for Canadian Libraries

Wanda Noel, BA, LLB

Published by
Canadian Library Association
Association pour l'avancement des sciences et des techniques de la documentation
1999

Canadian Cataloguing in Publication Data
Noel, Wanda
  Copyright guide for Canadian libraries

Co-published by Association pour l'avancement des sciences et
  des techniques de la documentation
ISBN 0-88802-294-8

  Copyright—Canada. 2. Libraries—Canada. I. Asted.
II. Canadian Library Association. III. Title.

KE2799.N63 1999   346.7104'82   C99-901589-3

Printed on recycled paper

The paper used in this publication meets the minimum requirements of American National Standard for Information Sciences—Permanence of Paper for Printed Library Materials, ANSI Z39.48-1984 ∞

Cover design: Beverly Bard
Photographs: girl with computer and girl with CD — Robert Llewellyn/SuperStock Inc.; piano — Charles Orrico/SuperStock Inc.; sheet music — Roderick Chen/SuperStock Inc. All others SuperStock Inc.

Wanda Noel, Barrister and Solicitor, 1389 Galetta Road, R.R. 2 Woodlawn, Ontario K0A 3M0
(613) 832-3136 Fax (613) 832-4066 wanda.noel@sympatico.ca

Copyright © 1999 Canadian Library Association and Wanda Noel
This guide has been prepared for members of the Canadian Library Association and ASTED. Members of the Canadian Library Association and ASTED only are authorized to reproduce this guide.
All other rights reserved.
ISBN 0-88802-294-8

Published by
Canadian Library Association
200 Elgin Street, Suite 602, Ottawa, Ontario K2P 1L5

Association pour l'avancement des sciences et des techniques de la documentation
3414, avenue du Parc, Bureau 202, Montréal, Québec H2X 2H5

Printed and bound in Canada

The publishers acknowledge the financial support of the Government of Canada through the Book Publishing Development Program for this project.